THE
DISTANCE
LEARNING
PLAYBOOK FOR
PARENTS

THE DISTANCE LEARNING PLAYBOOK FOR PARENTS

HOW TO SUPPORT YOUR CHILD'S ACADEMIC, SOCIAL, AND EMOTIONAL DEVELOPMENT IN ANY SETTING

ROSALIND WISEMAN · DOUGLAS FISHER
NANCY FREY · JOHN HATTIE

FOREWORD BY FORMER NATIONAL TEACHER
OF THE YEAR SARAH BROWN WESSLING

A SAGE Publishing Company

FOR INFORMATION:

Corwin

A SAGE Company

2455 Teller Road

Thousand Oaks, California 91320

(800) 233-9936

www.corwin.com

SAGE Publications Ltd.

1 Oliver's Yard

55 City Road

London EC1Y 1SP

United Kingdom

SAGE Publications India Pvt. Ltd.

B 1/I 1 Mohan Cooperative Industrial Area

Mathura Road, New Delhi 110 044

India

SAGE Publications Asia-Pacific Pte. Ltd.

18 Cross Street #10-10/11/12

China Square Central

Singapore 048423

Director and Publisher,
Corwin Classroom: Lisa Luedeke

Publisher: Jessica Allan

Editorial Development Manager: Julie Nemer

Associate Content
Development Editor: Sharon Wu

Production Editor: Melanie Birdsall

Copy Editor: Diane DiMura

Typesetter: C&M Digitals (P) Ltd.

Proofreader: Theresa Kay

Indexer: Sheila Hill

Cover Designer: Gail Buschman

Interior Designer: Scott Van Atta and Gail Buschman

Marketing Manager: Amanda Boudria

Section-opening images courtesy of iStock.com/Eoneren

Printed in the United States of America

ISBN 978-1-0718-3832-7

This book is printed on acid-free paper.

20 21 22 23 24 10 9 8 7 6 5 4 3 2 1

Contents

1 THE BASICS — 1

2 THE VALUE OF . . . — 15

online
resources

Visit the companion website at
resources.corwin.com/DLparents
for online and downloadable resources.

Foreword

Mornings at my house are the worst. If my three kids and I all get out the door on time, not forgetting anything, and with smiles on our faces, I pretty much feel like I've already won the day. But it rarely happens. Despite all my planning and best efforts, most mornings are chaotic, and I spend them trying to find any trick that might make them easier.

One day, amid my flurry to get all of us to school on time, my oldest son threatened to make the mornings even more turbulent than they already are. "Mom," Evan implored, "I need you to make me breakfast. I'm hungry by 9:30 and I don't eat lunch until 12:30. I really need a big breakfast in the mornings."

My anxiety rose. "I don't have time to make you breakfast, get everyone ready, and get to school on time. You know this. You're going to be sixteen soon. There's no reason you can't keep getting your own breakfast," I spat back.

"But Mom. I need a *big* breakfast. Like eggs or a protein smoothie. Something that gets me past 9:30 in the morning. Not cereal or toast."

I just looked at him without saying anything. In my mind, I was frantically trying to do the math. How long would this take me every morning? How much earlier would I need to get up each day? How many minutes would this take away from the hours I stole from the early morning to get ready to teach?

Before I said anything else, Evan hit me with a calm declaration: "I'm happy to do it myself, Mom. But you haven't taught me how to do it yet."

I hadn't taught him how to do it yet. Of course. I hadn't taught him how to do it yet because it was always just easier and more efficient for me to do it. I made less mess, fewer mistakes, could move faster around the kitchen by myself. His words stuck with me. By the time I got to my own high school English classroom, the weight of those words reverberated off the walls at school just as they had at home.

So often, our best intentions preclude the learning of others. Some of us are helpers or fixers by nature; others of us crave efficiency and control. Yet, we must give much of that up when we invite someone else to learn. As a teacher, this means I ask questions instead of giving answers. It means that instead of efficiency, I choose messy.

Teaching Evan how to make his own breakfasts would mean a time where the morning routine would take longer and create messes. He'd make mistakes I'd rather not have to clean up; however, *this is also precisely where the learning would happen.* Unless I invested in the mess now, I'd never release him to mastery and independence.

This lesson is as relevant today as it's ever been, for both teachers and parents. As we face a year where we'll experience an array of face-to-face, hybrid, online, and at-home learning configurations, the foundation we've known feels shaky. Yet this is also a powerful time to re-center ourselves on the importance of learning—what it really looks like and how we can foster it together. As parents, we don't have to be experts, but we do need to engage with our learners. Instead of worrying about having answers, we can ask our children to talk about their processes, ask them how they can find resources, and become curious about what they're *learning* instead of what they're *doing*. We can utilize the valuable practices and key mindframes described in this book, and help our children adopt them as well. As much as we crave efficiency amid the chaos, it's important for us to remember to take the time to model patience and curiosity amid uncertainty. This book will show you precisely how. In these pages, Rosalind, Doug, Nancy, and John explain how your children need to hear the adults they look up to saying things like, "It's okay to make mistakes and not get this on the first try," or "The mistakes are good because that means you are learning," or "I see that you did well on that test, and it's because you put in the extra effort and worked hard to take notes and reread the book," or "This makes me think about _____, what about you?" Parents don't have to be teachers, but they can be formidable influencers in helping their children learn to learn.

As a teacher, I need this lesson too. I can't expect my students to be able to learn independently before I've taught them how. Just because they've reached a certain age or grade level doesn't mean they've been taught *how* to solve that kind of problem, how to read that kind of text, how to make that kind of breakfast. I can't hand out assignments and pick them up and call that online learning. Instead, I need to focus on creating learning experiences, not tasks, for my students. As susceptible as I am right now to the pull of efficiency, I can't confuse that with the nuanced and individualized learning experience my students most need.

Our children have a part in this lesson as well. We need to teach them how to ask for help. We need to give them permission to be uncertain, confused, even frustrated. We need to model that frustration isn't failure; rather, it's a sign that learning is about to happen. We need to remind them that their parents aren't responsible for fixing the frustration, but we can listen with patience and curiosity as they figure it out.

Together, we are the ecosystem that will secure success for our students, our children, and ourselves this year. This book will help you see exactly what your part can look like. With their calm and reassuring advice, Rosalind Wiseman, Doug Fisher, Nancy Frey, and John Hattie help frame what's ahead and offer concrete, practical advice for creating family and classroom systems that enable our students to thrive.

And—in case you're curious—the time it took to teach my son *how* to make his own breakfasts instead of just *telling* him what to do has paid off. He's self-sufficient and less hungry—and he's taught his younger brother how to do it, too. The magic is in the mess, my friends.

—**Sarah Brown Wessling**, NBCT
English Teacher at Johnston High School, Former National
Teacher of the Year, and Laureate Emeritus for Teaching Channel

> PARENTS DON'T HAVE TO BE TEACHERS, BUT THEY CAN BE FORMIDABLE INFLUENCERS IN HELPING THEIR CHILDREN LEARN TO LEARN.

Dear Parent/Guardian,

In the midst of this global pandemic, we know that it may not be possible to have your child physically at school full time. We want nothing more than to bring your children back to our schools and engage them in meaningful learning activities. We miss your children. We miss those shared moments of success and the struggles that result in learning breakthroughs. We miss the smiles and watching social skills develop and unfold. We miss the opportunities to see your child play, learn, and grow. But we also want you to remember something very important: you are, and always will be, your child's first and primary teacher.

We will always be here to do our part—to do everything in our power to provide a robust education for your child. But more than ever, we need you. Over the years, we have come to know we can steadily rely on you to make sure your child comes to school on time, fed, clean, well-rested, and with completed homework in hand. We have welcomed with open arms your involvement in school activities, your desire to help run the PTA, your attendance at sporting and cultural events. But now we need you as partners on an even deeper level—as partners in learning and developing the language of learning, with us doing it together as a team.

We know that many of you have full-time employment or other stresses that may come with financial and housing difficulties, with the challenges of looking for work, caring for multiple children, or supporting other friends or family members in need. We also know you were not trained as teachers—that you love your kids but also sometimes admittedly realize they are just not enamored with schooling. We know our government made it compulsory for them to come to school—and that this was in part built around an assumption that as trained teachers we are, on average, better equipped that you may be to handle and navigate the role of educating your children. But this crisis has reminded us again just how valuable and irreplaceable your role is, too.

We are not asking you to become the teacher. We are asking you to partner with us however you are able and to support the learning opportunities we provide. We will continue to learn about what works in education and we will apply our best knowledge, the knowledge generated from decades of research, to build your child's social, emotional, and academic skills.

You are probably hearing a lot of talk about the lost learning during mid-2020 or about what some are calling the "COVID Slide." And there is even more talk about the loss of learning if students are not physically in school immediately. The fact of the matter is, we are teachers and our superpower is knowing where children are in their learning journey and supporting their continued growth. We did not forget how to teach. And our little secret is that about 50 percent of the instructional minutes in school are spent on things that students already know. Thus, this year, our task is to focus on what students need to learn and use the precious time we have with them to focus on that.

We also know that you all went to school and that after 15,000 hours in school, you too are experts and have strong views about school. Some of you did not have great experiences in schooling. Some of you had some brilliant teachers that changed your life course, but some of you missed these marvelous teachers. We realize that you, and our current society, expect much of schools, and schools attempt to solve many problems. Today's schools have a major focus on developing the skills of learning and on finding ways to teach students to work collectively in groups. Employers want graduates to know how to work in teams, to collaborate, to demonstrate high levels of empathy and respect for others, and to be able to "walk in the shoes of others." They want employees with high levels of respect for self and respect for others. We are good at developing these skills, but we need you too.

Acknowledgments

Corwin and the authors gratefully acknowledge the contributions of the following reviewers:

Barbara Buswell, MA
Executive Director, PEAK Parent Center

Gloria Ciriza, EdD
Assistant Superintendent, Instructional Services

Aiesha Eleusizov
Parent

Frederick Johnson, MD
Pediatrician

Farrah Lin
Parent

Sylvia Porras
Parent

David Sleet, PhD
Professor of Exercise and Nutritional Sciences
Former Director of the Division of Injury Prevention, Centers for Disease Control and Prevention

Cultures of Dignity teen editors Gus Kraft, Jake Chang, Radhika Khemka, Sara Davis, Trinidad Pavez, and the Cultures of Dignity Team who made our contribution to this book possible.

How to Use This Book

We want this guide to be as useful for you as possible. You might choose to read it from beginning to end; others might want to dip in and out of the sections that they're most interested in. The four sections provide information on different aspects of the distance learning experience.

We begin this resource focused on the basics. Household routines have been upended and finding balance has been a challenge due to external and internal stressors. We make recommendations for creating learning environments and routines. We provide ideas for supporting your child's engagement with the school and its teachers. And, importantly, we remind you to take care of yourself.

The second section focuses on what you can do to help your child learn. We share ideas that can help keep learning at the center and suggest ways to maximize the time that teachers are engaged with your child. We try very hard to provide information and ideas in ways that are not overwhelming for you or your child. After all, the teachers will be working to ensure that your child is learning. Select the ones that are tailored to your family and your child. These are organized as quick reference guides:

➡ **What is it?** A short definition of the concept

➡ **Why is it important?** A brief discussion of its role in learning

➡ **Why is it important in distance learning?** The value of this as a home support for distance learning

➡ **Take action:** Suggestions for ways to implement it

➡ **Key messages:** Short summary statements to capture the main points

The third part focuses on your child's well-being. Academics are important, but so is social and emotional development. We know that you are concerned about your child's socialization and social skills. And we know that every parent wants their child to develop productive, healthy relationships with others. These are organized similarly to the previous section and include some landmines to watch out for.

The final section of this resource focuses on the mindsets for your children and your family—mindframes that will serve them well long after the current crisis has ended. Each of these is a brief principle that serves you and your family well, along with key messages. Yes, your child will likely return to physical schooling. But the lessons we learn now should change the ways that schools work. The values, principles, and mind-sets we share in this book extend well beyond the pandemic teaching that is currently necessary. They are ways of us working together to better the lives of children.

We thank you for your partnership. Together, we know we will get through this.

Hold Up! Please Read This!

Before you dive into distance learning, that is, the reason you bought this book, we would like to create the learning space with you. We believe that learning happens best when we are clear about our principles, the beliefs that guide our actions. Here are some guiding principles to consider as you engage in your own learning. (And by the way, they work really well with young people too!)

➡ Everyone deserves to be treated with dignity.

➡ No one knows everything; together we know a lot.

➡ Creating space for participation and contribution makes everyone feel valued.

➡ Engaging curiosity, especially when we're uncomfortable, is the key to learning.

➡ Seeking meaningful connection gives our lives purpose.

➡ Acknowledge that conflict is inevitable and collaboration is essential to resolution.

➡ Accepting feedback is invaluable to personal growth.

➡ Be easy on people, but hard on ideas. This allows people to make mistakes while applying rigorous analysis to our ideas and beliefs.

➡ Listening is being prepared to be changed by what you hear.

➡ Every child deserves a great teacher not by chance but by design.

These are the norms that we hope you will carry with you as you engage with the ideas in this book, support your child, and interact with teachers.

Distance, Remote, and Blended Learning

You're probably hearing a lot of terms used to describe the ways that schools can operate given the mandates around limiting physical contact and carefully monitoring attendance in the building. There is no one "right way" for school systems to address these issues and implement some combination of distance, hybrid, and/or in-person schooling, but there are wrong ways. Thankfully, there are decades of research on these models of providing schooling. Of course, none of these studies occurred when entire systems were closed. But we can still draw on the evidence collected to make recommendations.

It might comfort you to know that the research tells us teaching from a distance is not necessarily more ineffective than teaching in person. It turns out that distance learning has what we call a very low "effect size." Effect sizes are ways to measure the impact or magnitude of something. It's rather like the scale we use to measure the impact of earthquakes. Some you don't feel; others are powerful. Research says that distance learning is not even a tremor. But we need to be careful when we analyze that research. In this case, a low effect size suggests that the setting isn't the deciding factor: in-person or distance learning is not better or worse. It should not be interpreted that "distance is disastrous." In fact, some students really excel when learning from a distance.

What matters then? It turns out, what we *do* matters rather than the medium. To be sure, what we witnessed in mid-2020 was not distance learning. It was pandemic teaching, crisis teaching, or "quaranteaching." Like most professions, we had to pivot and there was a steep learning curve. But we know more now. And, as the late Maya Angelou said, *Do the best you can until you know better. Then, when you know better, do better*. And now we know better.

To continue on effect sizes, it turns out that interactive videos are a powerful accelerator for learning. So are intelligent tutoring systems and teacher–student relationships. We could go on, but we'll save that for the second section of this book. One of the lowest effect sizes related to technology is the presence of mobile phones. Turn them off. Yes, that's our first recommendation for your child's learning. When your child is engaged in learning tasks, phones should be off and not a distraction from the learning. [As a note, some of the young people who reviewed this for us might not appreciate us telling you this, even though they agreed that their smartphones were a distraction from their learning.]

In terms of formats for distance learning, there really is no evidence about what works best. Some school districts are fully online. Others are reducing the hours students are physically present. Others have created alternating day schedules. Still others have morning and afternoon split schedules. We have heard of schedules in which students are on campus one week and then off the next. Another variation of that proposed that students who were on campus for four days would then be off for ten to ensure that there was time to determine if anyone was exposed to COVID-19. We have also heard about pods of students staying together and then shutting down if someone is sick or exposed. And we have heard about groups of parents coming together in a neighborhood and having one person host all the children. These might all work. We don't yet know. We do know that there will be fewer minutes "live" with students and some time spent on learning tasks without the teacher present. Most states have revised their instructional minute requirements to accommodate distance learning.

We also know that you are likely to be disappointed in some of the decisions that your school system makes. You have that right and you should share your ideas and opinions with school leaders. But for the sake of your children, try to refrain from criticizing the decisions in front of them. They will pick up on your disappointment and it may just compromise the learning your child is able to do. We know that lack of confidence in the teacher is harmful to learning; the negative impact on the child when a parent believes that the teacher is ineffective is nearly off the charts.

WHEN YOUR CHILD IS ENGAGED IN LEARNING TASKS, PHONES SHOULD BE OFF AND NOT A DISTRACTION FROM THE LEARNING.

We are concerned about equity. At this time, we all need to do what we can. School systems are focused on ensuring all students have access to technology and food. If you can afford a computer for your child, provide it. It may help stretch the school system budget so that other families can have computers. If you are able to support your child's learning during times that the class is not meeting together, please do so. That may save a little time for the teacher to spend with a child whose family is not able to do so. If you have time, please volunteer to be a tutor or mentor or classroom aide. This will allow essential workers to do their jobs with a little more peace of mind.

In sum, distance learning is not going to harm your child's education if there is a partnership between you, your child, and the teacher. Let the teacher teach. Support your child's sense of purpose in their education. Implement some of the recommendations in each of the section of this book. You may have to be more involved that you were in the past, but don't assume that you have to provide most of the instruction your child needs. And yes, things will get messy, there will be moments of frustration, and maybe even times when you or your child wants to give up. All these feelings and more are understandable, and this book will help you get through those moments so that you and your child can get their education back on track with your relationship stronger in the process.

1 THE BASICS

We call this section "The Basics" for a reason. The basics are critical to building the foundation you need for your child's education. You will find some essential actions that parents, students, and teachers have found useful on the journey to ensure learning still happens away from the place called school. We think of these as the enabling conditions that will allow the values and mindsets we describe to take root. Having said that, remember that these are recommendations, not requirements. You know your child best. It's not worth a dramatic battle to implement all these recommendations. We care that your child wants to learn and knows *how* to learn way more than we care if your child complies with the general ideas collected from others.

In this section:

- [ ] ESTABLISH ROUTINES
- [ ] CREATE A LEARNING ENVIRONMENT
- [ ] LEARN THE LEARNING MANAGEMENT SYSTEM
- [ ] FOLLOW ZOOM ETIQUETTE
- [ ] ENSURE THAT YOUR CHILDREN SLEEP
- [ ] MONITOR SCREEN TIME
- [ ] COMMUNICATE WITH TEACHERS
- [ ] TAKE CARE OF YOURSELF

ESTABLISH ROUTINES

When your child attended physical school, there were any number of routines that she engaged in on a daily and weekly basis. There was a time to get up. There was tooth brushing, hair combing, and eating breakfast—all to be done by a certain time every day. There was getting ready for school. There was coming home from school. Each family has a way of accomplishing these things. In many families, that all fell apart in the pandemic. Students were showing up to virtual school not having eaten, not looking groomed, and even sleepy.

One of the best practices we can enact during distance learning is to establish routines for children. It's comforting and predictable. And predicable routines are known to reduce stress. Over time, these become habits that don't take any cognitive energy.

YOU KNOW YOUR CHILD BEST. IT'S NOT WORTH A DRAMATIC BATTLE TO IMPLEMENT ALL THESE RECOMMENDATIONS.

We cannot tell you the best time in your family to ensure that children wake up, bathe, brush their teeth, eat, and complete the range of personal care tasks required for hygiene and health. What we can tell you is that if you create a schedule and follow it, your quality of life will increase, and the stress level of your children will decrease.

It's important that children feel like they are going to school, even when they are learning from a distance. It's a mindset that we're looking for. And when they are ready for school, and look like they are ready for school, they're a little less worried about appearing online. If your routines have fallen apart a bit, we recommend developing a written schedule for the major tasks that need to be completed, appropriate for the age of the child, of course. Even consider making lunch the night before if that was your habit previously. It sends the message that tomorrow is a school day. And, figure out which alarm clock system will work for your family and an agreed accountability strategy if someone oversleeps.

For example, in the Johnson family, they created a bathroom checklist for their three children, ages 5, 7, and 10. As Matt said, "I know it sounds silly and that we should have thought about it on our own, but when we created the checklist it took away some of the conflict in our family. We used to fight about these things. Now, we check the list and only focus on things that didn't get done." After four weeks of the checklist, habits had been formed and they didn't need to use it any longer.

As part of the routines, remember that chores are also important as they instill responsibility in young people. They teach responsibility, self-reliance, teamwork, time management, respect, and help build a work ethic. When we were young, none of us remember really liking our chores, but we do remember the sense of accomplishment we experienced when they were completed. Children need to learn that their investment in the household benefits everyone.

Consider the routines that are important for your family to function and the habits you want to build in your children. These are the key messages:

 Identify the self-care needs of your children and develop routines for them to accomplish the tasks.

➡ Develop a schedule, if needed, for your children to follow the routines.

➡ Make sure that your children are ready for school each day.

➡ Develop a list of chores that children need to complete.

➡ Avoid negotiating schoolwork versus chores.

CREATE A LEARNING ENVIRONMENT

We all need a place to work and learn. For most school-age children, that has been in the school building and perhaps a kitchen table or small desk in their room. Learning at home heightens the need for a consistent and convenient place for children to engage in schooling. We'll start with the ideal and then consider some options.

Ideally, each child will have a location that is "theirs" to work. Ideally, this will not be in their bedroom (and really not on their bed) as their peers, teachers, and adults in the homes of other students do not need to be inside your child's room. We recognize that the ideal is not always possible. But, ideally, there is a location in which each child has a dedicated space. They do not need to be alone in that space. In fact, it may be better socially for them to spend time together during the day while learning. But they do need a place to keep their things. For example, you might provide your child a bin to hold books, workbooks, note-books, journals, and other school supplies (crayons, pencils, scissors, etc.).

For example, there are four people in the Green's home. They decided to convert their dining room, which they rarely used, into a shared workspace. Two adults and two children each have desks in there, and they use headphones while on video calls, much like is done in a call center. As Jeremy, their fourth grader, said, "When Dad is on his calls, we try to be quiet and do our work. And he tries to be quiet when I am in class with Ms. Montez. We all have work to do." His second-grade sister Sarah said, "We all go to work together after breakfast but sometimes I go outside for class." In the Green's home, there is a small fenced yard with a picnic table that has a sun umbrella, and Sarah likes to work there.

Jessica is a single parent of two teenagers. They decided to convert their garage into an office space. As Jessica said, "It turns out that they really liked the project of trans-forming the garage. They took pictures and documented the whole thing. They created a really cool space for their studies. I have to work outside the home, and I like to check in on them while they're in their new offices."

Of course, space is a premium and not all families have garages or dining rooms. We'll take what we can get. These are the key messages:

➡ Identify a dedicated workspace for each child, ideally outside of their bedroom.

➡ Try to keep the space consistent so that habits form relative to that space.

➡ Keep the supplies needed for learning in that space.

➡ Develop plans for taking breaks, movement, and getting water or food.

➡ Establish ground rules for using the space, including how others in the home should act in that space.

➡ Ask them to leave that space to do other things, such as exercise, eat, and socialize.

LEARN THE LEARNING MANAGEMENT SYSTEM

There are a number of systems that schools use to deliver instruction and learning tasks for students. These are generically known as learning management systems (LMS). Examples include Microsoft Teams, Google Classroom, Canvas, Blackboard, Edmodo, and so on. Each of them has unique features. To maximize your child's learning, you'll want to be familiar with the system that your school district has selected.

To start with, you'll need to know your child's login process. Some school systems have a single sign-in procedure whereas others have different processes. Just like you would with your bank information, make sure that your child's passwords are secure. There has been more than one example of a student logging in as another and engaging in some questionable, and even significantly problematic, behaviors. You may want to consider something like 1password (1password.com), which is a system that securely stores and manages passwords.

Next, you'll want to explore the ways in which the LMS works. How do learners navigate through the site? How it is organized? How do they submit work? It's hard to help your child when they are stuck and frustrated if you are not sure about the system. Learning the system in a high-stress situation is a recipe for conflict and frustration.

Some systems allow for customization such as size of the fonts used or the activation of speech recognition software. If you are not sure about the customization features, feel free to ask the teacher. These systems are developing rapidly, and you don't want to miss any features that could aid in your child's learning.

The LMS will be one of the primary ways that your child will access content and tasks. It's wise to have a general understanding about the way it works. These are the key messages:

➡ Find out how to log into the learning management system.

➡ Make sure that the passwords your child uses are secure.

➡ Learn the features of the learning management system so that you can help your child as needed.

➡ Find out the protocols for how your child submits assignments, asks the teacher a question about an assignment, or what to do if an assignment is "missing" when your child has turned it in. Again, don't wait for your child to have these experiences!

FOLLOW ZOOM ETIQUETTE

Not all school systems use the Zoom tool for video conferencing, but there is a growing trend to call it zoom etiquette irrespective of which platform is used. Your child may be in Microsoft Teams, Google Meet, or another system. Regardless, there are certain behaviors that are expected when children are in a synchronous situation in which they are "in class" live with the teacher and other students. (**Synchronous** is distance learning that happens in real time during live sessions. **Asynchronous** learning is distance learning that happens apart from the class when students complete tasks at their own pace.)

Teachers have expectations for students in their classes, whether they are taught in person or online. Teachers should make those expectations explicit for your child at the beginning of the school year. During distance learning, teachers may need your help in getting students to practice these expectations. Of course, the expectations vary by grade and teacher, but there are some general guidelines that are always useful. For example, it's important that your child has their materials ready before the meeting so they can join the session on time. In fact, they should be ready five minutes before class starts. As the saying goes, early is on time. It's frustrating, time consuming, and visually awkward to have a child leave the session to go get something or to have them join late. Not to obsess on time, but you want to take advantage of as much time with the teacher as possible.

It's useful for your child to stay in one spot during the meeting. If you were able to establish a consistent work area for your child, this will pay dividends when they are in live sessions with their class. Please don't allow your child to walk around the house while in a video meeting. It's really hard for the teacher to focus, and classmates will be distracted by watching various parts of your home. Remember, too, that the class can see into your home so checking out the visual field of the camera, based on where the computer is sitting, is important.

Some systems allow for virtual backgrounds. If backgrounds are allowed, they should be appropriate for school. We find them useful to drown out the distractions of seeing into the home. Other students are less likely to ask questions about what they see in the room if there is a background. Some schools even provide virtual backgrounds with school mascots or a photo of the classroom so that all of the backgrounds look the same.

Make sure your child knows when to mute. When there is background noise in the environment, students should know to mute their sound. They should also know how to unmute to answer questions and interact with peers. Please help your child by not vacuuming or engaging in other really noisy tasks, if at all possible. Encourage your child to keep the camera on. It's so much better for the teacher to see faces. Not only does it help with the student–teacher relationship, visual cues let the teacher know if the child is understanding the lesson or not. It's also important for building a sense of community in the class.

ENCOURAGE YOUR CHILD TO KEEP THE CAMERA ON. IT'S SO MUCH BETTER FOR THE TEACHER TO SEE FACES.

TEACH YOUR CHILD HOW TO TURN OFF THE SELF-VIEW FEATURE SO THAT THEY AREN'T FORCED TO LOOK AT THEMSELVES ALL DAY. WHEN THEY LEARN TO DO SO, STUDENTS REPORT THAT THEY ARE MUCH MORE LIKELY TO KEEP THEIR CAMERAS ON.

We recognize that some students do not like to keep looking at themselves on camera. They may be self-conscious or uncomfortable. After all, we're not accustomed to looking at ourselves for hours on end, and most young people use filters and apps to adjust the photos that they post. We suggest that you teach your child how to turn off the self-view feature so that they aren't forced to look at themselves all day. Others can still see them, but they don't have to watch themselves. When they learn to do so, students report that they are much more likely to keep their cameras on.

There are also a number of tools that children need to learn to use. They can virtually raise their hands or use features that allow them to indicate that they want to join in conversation or ask questions. There are ways for them to join the conversation, such as the chat feature.

And, it should go without saying, these live sessions are class time and thus children and youth need to treat each other with respect. That includes chat. If your child tells you something that is problematic, say something. If it's dangerous, you may need to interrupt the class. If not, you can let the teacher know following the session. Having said that, we do believe that young people deserve some privacy in their learning. Parents, please avoid hovering over every lesson. It will make your child anxious and you may inadvertently criticize something in front of your child. Your child needs to make mistakes, interact with others, and learn to attend, all of which may be thwarted if you are watching everything that they do.

Jessica and John Hannigan, developers of the PBIS Champion Model System, created the SOAR Virtual Learning Matrix to demonstrate expectations for live sessions (see the figure on the facing page). They emphasize the importance of students taking control of their own actions, staying organized, and showing respect during virtual learning sessions.

Remember, your child's behavior is on display for all of the other parents who have children in the class. That's not the norm in physical school, which is why it's another reason to reinforce the etiquette aspects of live lessons. These are key messages:

➡ Know the teacher expectations and support them.

➡ As part of the routines discussed above, make sure that your child knows the schedule for live sessions.

➡ Encourage your child to use the camera. Show them the option to hide the self-view if that alleviates anxiety.

➡ For the first several live sessions, take note of your child's actions. Was the mute function used appropriately? Was your child respectful? Monitor the live sessions periodically but avoid the temptation to hover.

➡ Talk with your child about the live sessions and their behavior and actions. Encourage your child to reflect on their participation and learning.

S.O.A.R. *VIRTUAL LEARNING MATRIX*

S — SELF-CONTROL

- Follow instructions
- Wait for your turn to speak or contribute
- Use the raise-your-hand feature
- Minimize distractions
- Utilize chat features appropriately

O — ON-TASK

- Log in on time
- Be present/actively engaged
- Organize your materials
- Set daily goals
- Make yourself visible
- Have a backup plan if you get disconnected

A — ACHIEVEMENT

- Complete tasks on time/stay on top of assignments
- Be prepared
- Complete preparation work
- Reach out to the teacher for help
- Share and collaborate
- Write in complete sentences
- Create a schedule/space to complete assignments

R — RESPECT

- Mute microphone when others are speaking
- Respect others' perspectives
- Use kind words
- Use proper text etiquette (ALL CAPS, bold, italics, sarcasm/jokes, etc. can be misinterpreted in a digital space)
- Help each other during group assignments and in designated meeting rooms
- Resolve conflict peacefully

EQUITY
in school
discipline

PBIS Rewards.
PBISrewards.com

Source: Courtesy of Jessica and John Hannigan.

ENSURE THAT YOUR CHILDREN SLEEP

To sleep, perchance to dream. Yes, that's a fragment of the Shakespeare quote, but it's the part that gives us hope. Sleep is important. It's as important as food, water, and physical and emotional safety. There is evidence that an extreme lack of sleep contributes to behavior problems, mood disturbances, emotional instability, and even obesity. In terms of the research, lack of sleep is one of the few things that has a definite negative effect size, or impact, on children's learning.

There are two interesting outcomes from school closures. Some people are sleeping more, which is good—to a point. But some people, especially children, are not sleeping in a predictable pattern, which is not good.

Speaking of adolescents, there is some folklore that their natural circadian rhythms require that they go to sleep later and wake up later. To a point, that is true. Experts suggest that it is about an hour difference. The other shifts in their desire to go to sleep late are more social in nature. Importantly, teenagers need more sleep than adults. The National Sleep Foundation examined the research and gathered experts from the fields of psychology, anatomy and physiology, as well as from pediatrics, neurology, gerontology, and gynecology to reach a consensus. These are their recommendations:

SIMPLY SAID, CHILDREN WHO DO NOT GET SUFFICIENT SLEEP LEARN LESS.

Age	Recommended	May be appropriate	Not recommended
Newborns *0–3 months*	14 to 17 hours	11 to 13 hours 18 to 19 hours	Less than 11 hours More than 19 hours
Infants *4–11 months*	12 to 15 hours	10 to 11 hours 16 to 18 hours	Less than 10 hours More than 18 hours
Toddlers *1–2 years*	11 to 14 hours	9 to 10 hours 15 to 16 hours	Less than 9 hours More than 16 hours
Preschoolers *3–5 years*	10 to 13 hours	8 to 9 hours 14 hours	Less than 8 hours More than 14 hours
School-Age Children *6–13 years*	9 to 11 hours	7 to 8 hours 12 hours	Less than 7 hours More than 12 hours
Teenagers *14–17 years*	8 to 10 hours	7 hours 11 hours	Less than 7 hours More than 11 hours
Young Adults *18–25 years*	7 to 9 hours	6 hours 10 to 11 hours	Less than 6 hours More than 11 hours
Adults *26–64 years*	7 to 9 hours	6 hours 10 hours	Less than 6 hours More than 10 hours
Older Adults *≥65 years*	7 to 8 hours	5 to 6 hours 9 hours	Less than 5 hours More than 9 hours

Source: Adapted from Sleep Foundation (www.sleepfoundation.org).

As we noted earlier, routines are important. Sleep routines are especially important. To avoid a dramatic scene every night that results in tantrums (younger children) or highly irritating arguments (older children and teens), create an evening routine. Ensure that the TV and all tech devices are off at least one hour before bedtime. (A lot of online bullying occurs in the hour before and after lights-out.) We recognize that impacts you as well, but it is critical for quality sleep. Blue light can be stimulating and thus prevent our brains from sleeping (and there are special glasses and screen protectors that you can purchase to reduce the strain from this light during the day). As part of the bedtime routine for younger children, engage in the same quiet activities each night, such as reading a book together, singing songs, completing a task—just make it familiar and routine. For older children, set expectations and be aware of their use of technology in their bedrooms after they have supposedly gone to bed. Some families have found success by instituting a routine about collecting devices at bedtime and keeping them in the parent's bedroom until the following morning.

If your child is not getting enough sleep or is going to bed too late, develop a ten-day plan to improve this. It's too hard to suddenly change the bedtime as your child is likely to lay in bed unable to sleep. Instead, identify the number of minutes gap between the ideal time and the current time (for example, 8 p.m. versus 10 p.m.). That's 120 minutes. Divide by 10 and move back bedtime by that amount each night.

Sleep, both in terms of quantity and quality, is an important yet often neglected aspect of schooling. Simply said, children who do not get sufficient sleep learn less. These are the key messages:

LACK OF SLEEP IS ONE OF THE FEW THINGS THAT HAS A DEFINITE NEGATIVE EFFECT.

➡ Sleep impacts learning.

➡ Add nighttime activities and expectations to your list of routines.

➡ Establish bedtimes and stick to them.

➡ Avoid electronics that emit blue light one hour before bedtime.

➡ If necessary, keep a sleep journal, or ask your child to do one for two weeks, to determine if your child is getting enough sleep.

MONITOR SCREEN TIME

It seems strange to discuss monitoring screen time, when distance learning demands more screen time—but this is the point—monitor for best use of screen time noting that now even more time is spent on devices.

There is some debate about how much time children and youth should spend looking at a screen. The same debate raged decades ago about TV. We know that they should not be on screens the hour before sleeping. But what about the total number of hours that are acceptable? Distance learning requires that children spend more time looking at a screen. And this is in addition to the amount of time that they are looking at a screen for entertainment or social purposes. The World Health Organization suggests that children under five have no more than one hour per day of screen time. But after that, the recommendations are murky.

Perhaps it is less about the number of minutes and more about the tasks that students are doing. And perhaps it is important to consider the things that are not done when students are always on a device. Are they playing? Are they interacting with others? What about art projects? Do they do their chores? Do they talk with family members? In sum, there is no clear evidence about how many minutes of screen time a child should have. However, the two extremes of laissez-faire and digital teetotalism are not helpful, especially if we want students to learn from a distance. A good rule might be to ensure that your child spends as much time doing something active or productive off a device as they do on a device.

A few facts come to mind as we focus on screen time. First, not all programs and apps are educationally sound. There is a vast knowledge base about learning, specifically about how people learn. Some programs and apps are designed in a way that is consistent with this evidence and others are not. Look for recommendations from educators about which apps are likely to impact your child's skill and concept development. For example, codeSpark Academy is highly rated by parents and educators as a tool useful in teaching coding.

Second, children should take breaks away from the screen. In part, it's good for their eyes. And in part, it's good to get them doing other things and not sitting down. Look at the schedule of events for the week and identify times when your child can take a break from the screen and do something else. If at all possible, get them to move. Sitting in a chair all day is really not good for any of us.

Third, for complex texts and tasks, the brain prefers paper. Your child's reading should not be limited to that which happens on a screen. You may be thinking about your own reading using a device. It's likely that you are reading things that you can easily read. And you probably have some topics or text types that you learn more from when they are on paper. In general, readers gain general understanding from digital texts but fewer of the key details. Just consider how many times you have responded to an email asking for information that was already in the previous message. How often do you get digital flyers or messages from your child's school and forget about the details (where, what time, what to bring)? Having a flyer printed out and then hanging it on the fridge allows us to go back and keep track. Speaking of reading, as we will discuss in the next section, your child reads about 90 minutes per day at school. Ask yourself, how much reading is my child doing at home?

Thus, it seems reasonable to suggest that synchronous sessions need to be conducted via technology and that some learning tasks can be completed via the online learning management system. Other tasks do not require technology. It's important to recognize that your child's eyes should be away from the technology on a regular basis. These are the key messages:

> ➡ Technology and screen time are not inherently bad or good.
> ➡ There are effective apps that facilitate learning, but not all of them do so.
> ➡ You should schedule regular tech breaks and ensure that your child does something other than look at a device.
> ➡ Make sure that your child has some reading material and tasks that are printed on old-school paper.

FOR COMPLEX TEXTS AND TASKS, THE BRAIN PREFERS PAPER.

COMMUNICATE WITH TEACHERS

Think of your child's teacher as your partner. You are in this together. You do not need to be a subject matter expert of every academic specialty. We are not asking you to teach chemistry, algebraic thinking, phonics, or how to write an argumentative speech, even though you might be able to. The teacher is still the teacher. In studies of parent frustration regarding distance learning in 2020, it was common for family members to note that they needed more communication from their children's teachers regarding schedules, tasks, and assignments. They also wanted their children to receive more feedback from the teacher and to spend more time with the teacher. So, let's focus on the communication. Teachers should send weekly schedules in advance. You should know when your child is expected to be present for live sessions and what the workflow is for the week. Let's focus on the quality and timing of the contact between teachers and parents.

We believe that your child, and by extension you, should be able to answer three basic questions for each learning experience:

➡ **What am I learning today?** This is the content that students need to master.

➡ **Why am I learning it?** This is the relevance of the lesson.

➡ **How will I know that I have learned it?** This is the criteria that can be used to determine success.

If lessons are random collections of tasks, children are less likely to engage and thus learn. If the teacher does not make the answers to these questions clear, feel free to ask for clarification in a kind way. If you don't get a satisfactory answer, you might have to step in and help your child figure out the answers to these questions. They really are that important.

Talk to your child more about their learning than what they are "doing." Welcome their struggles, their grappling with the ideas, because learning wasn't meant to be easy. Any indication it is, is conveying to your child that they are not smart, not able, and denies them the learning that learning is hard work.

> **TALK TO YOUR CHILD MORE ABOUT THEIR LEARNING THAN WHAT THEY ARE "DOING."**

Partnerships require strong communication to be effective. As such, you should establish a communication plan with your child's teacher. Ask the teacher how they prefer the communication to work. Emails? Messages in the learning management system? Some teachers use one-way messaging systems and others provide cell phone numbers. There is no one right way, but try to honor the communication system that the teacher prefers.

We encourage you to communicate with the teacher on a weekly basis (younger children) and to teach your child to reach out to teachers with questions (teens). That's not to say you end your responsibility to monitor your child's learning when they turn thirteen, but rather that they learn to accept some responsibility. Of course, you'll still monitor their attendance and task completion. During distance learning, teachers are typically provided additional time for planning and communicating. It's important that you know the expectations, know how your child is doing, and know what you can do to help. Again, you're not the teacher but you are an important part of the system that will ensure your child learns.

And, please remember that the teacher is human. The teacher is also working from home and may have many stressors in their life. Some teachers have small children at home; others have elderly family members. We are all in this together and we will get through this, together. However, if you feel that your child's needs are not being met after communicating regularly, first contact the teacher expressing your concerns through the mode of communication that the teacher has requested. If you don't receive a response or feel their response is inadequate, you should feel free to attend the office hours of the principal or send a quick message requesting a conversation. This is not intended to get the teacher in trouble but rather to address any misunderstandings and get things back on track.

You may need to be a bit more active in your child's education during these times. As parent.com notes, *parent* is a verb. Teachers and parents need each other. These are the key messages:

➡ Remember, you do not have to be "the teacher" to ensure that your child learns.

➡ If not provided, ask for a weekly schedule so that you can build routines around it.

➡ Make sure your child knows what is to be learned, why they are learning it, and when they will know they have achieved success.

➡ Develop a communication system with the teacher(s).

➡ Be involved in your child's education.

TAKE CARE OF YOURSELF

Yes, you read that right. You can't fill your child's cup if yours is empty. Remember the last time you were on an airplane? The flight attendant gave you some good advice: Put your oxygen mask on first before helping others. Please don't stop reading this book. It's important. Your child needs you.

Remember the section about routines? That applies to you as well. You probably don't need a reminder to brush your teeth, but having a morning routine and an evening routine, and a routine to signal that work is done for the day, are protective actions you can take to ward off stress. The same is true for sleeping. It's protective, even though it feels like some days you don't have time to sleep. And a place to work? Yep. If you work in the home, you need a dedicated space as well. Taking breaks? Absolutely.

In addition, it's important to note that exercise and nutrition are important factors that can reduce stress. And teachers need you healthy so that we can collaborate with you and ensure your child learns. Take time for yourself each day. And make sure you have at least one meaningful conversation each day with someone outside of your home.

These are the key messages:

➡ Develop a life-work balance plan.

➡ Keep a dedicated workspace.

➡ Set ground rules with the people in your space.

➡ Create a morning routine.

➡ Maintain regular hours, including sleep hours.

➡ Schedule breaks.

➡ End your day with a routine.

➡ Socialize with colleagues.

➡ Have a meaningful conversation each day with someone outside of your home.

➡ Develop a healthy self-plan that includes nutrition and exercise.

This is so important, and we really hope you'll give it a try. In fact, it's so important that we recommend you have a commitment or accountability partner. Here's a tool you can use to hold yourself accountable (a downloadable copy is also available on the companion website):

My commitment partner is	
I need the following from this person	
We will check in	☐ Daily ☐ Two times per week ☐ Three times per week ☐ Weekly ☐ Bi-weekly

online resources 🔖 Available for download at **resources.corwin.com/DLparents**

If, despite your efforts, you continue to struggle, seek the help of professionals who can support you in your personal well-being. Again, your child needs you and we want you to be healthy and happy.

2 THE VALUE OF . . .

Your time is valuable. We are not asking you to be the teacher, but instead to partner with us in very strategic ways so we can get a return on our investment in your child's learning. The research already tells us much about what works in education. It leads us back, time and again, to tried and true methods, and points us to solid, foundational ideas we can tap into that have a high likelihood of impacting your child's learning in a positive way.

In this section:

- ☐ READING VOLUME
- ☐ READING WIDELY
- ☐ READING ALOUD
- ☐ VOCABULARY GAMES
- ☐ ORAL LANGUAGE DEVELOPMENT
- ☐ FOUNDATIONAL READING SKILLS: PHONEMIC AWARENESS
- ☐ FOUNDATIONAL READING SKILLS: ALPHABETICS AND PHONICS
- ☐ FOUNDATIONAL READING SKILLS: FLUENCY

- ☐ WRITING ACROSS THE DAY
- ☐ SCAFFOLDED WRITING EXPERIENCES
- ☐ MATHEMATICS ACROSS THE DAY
- ☐ SUPPLEMENTAL MATHEMATICS INSTRUCTION
- ☐ ARTS AND MUSIC
- ☐ GUIDING, NOT TELLING
- ☐ WAIT TIME
- ☐ PRACTICE

We present these ideas, the low-hanging fruit of what we already know will influence your child's learning for the better, so that you can immediately hit the ground running and extend the learning your child does at home. Don't feel that you have to do them all! Maybe this analogy will help: This is not a plated dinner; it's a buffet. Choose the things that you like and that you can do. Talk with your child so that they can talk to the teacher and ask which of these things will be most complimentary to the learning your child is doing with them. And above all, don't stress. The goal is simply to have your child engaged in learning as much as possible. Here's a comparison of the roles:

> DON'T FEEL THAT YOU HAVE TO DO THEM ALL! CHOOSE THE THINGS THAT YOU LIKE AND THAT YOU CAN DO.

Teacher	Parent/Family
• Rigorous	• LOVE
• Intensive	• Bonding and connectedness
• Standards-based instruction	• Fun and games
• Developmentally progressive	• Supportive of the instruction
• Productive struggle	• Doesn't feel like school
• Growth-producing relationship	• Brings the family together in warm, positive ways

THE VALUE OF READING VOLUME

What is it?

The number of minutes that eyes are on texts adds up to the total volume of reading that someone does. Lots of reading, referred to as reading volume, builds general knowledge and reading proficiency. In terms of effect sizes, reading volume has a respectable impact on student learning. Unfortunately, there is evidence that reading volume was decreasing even before the pandemic. In 2016, 16 percent of students reported reading a book or magazine for pleasure compared with 60 percent in 1976. It's just gotten worse during the most recent crisis.

Why is it important?

Children learn about the world in many different ways. The experiences they have and the conversations they have with you are important. Much of the academic knowledge needed for school success comes through reading. The number of rare words, which are words uncommon in speech but present in reading, include many of the academic concepts that are taught in school. A great study on the use of rare words in books and in adult speech found something pretty amazing. The researchers found that children's books contained an average of 30.9 rare words per thousand, and comic books were even higher—53.5 per thousand. In conversations between college graduates, the number was much lower at 17.3 rare words per thousand. That's because our spoken language is different from our written language. Your child's independent reading provides them with exposure to richer vocabulary and knowledge.

Here's another reason why the amount of reading matters: Students who read more outside of school score better on standardized reading tests. There is a correlation, or relationship, between the amount of reading they do and their achievement. A large study of the reading habits of elementary students found that those who read for 15 minutes a day beyond their schoolwork read an average of 1,168,000 words a year and reliably scored at the 70th percentile on reading assessments. The numbers increase with every minute of outside reading: Those who read for 65 minutes a day read an additional 4,733,000 words a year and scored at the 98th percentile! Here's the very best news of all: Reading anything counts! Comic books, joke books, graphic novels, narrative stories, books about video games and sports, and informational texts—it all counts (see Figure 1).

> THE RESEARCHERS FOUND THAT CHILDREN'S BOOKS CONTAINED AN AVERAGE OF 30.9 RARE WORDS PER THOUSAND, AND COMIC BOOKS WERE EVEN HIGHER—53.5 PER THOUSAND.

1 RELATIONSHIP BETWEEN READING VOLUME AND ACHIEVEMENT

Percentile Rank[a]	Minutes of Reading per Day			Words Read per Year	
	Books	Text[b]	All Reading[c]	Books	Text[b]
98	65.0	67.3	90.7	4,358,000	4,733,000
90	21.1	33.4	40.4	1,823,000	2,357,000
80	14.2	24.6	31.1	1,146,000	1,697,000
70	9.6	16.9	21.7	622,000	1,168,000
60	6.5	13.1	18.1	432,000	722,000
50	4.6	9.2	12.9	282,000	601,000
40	3.2	6.2	8.6	200,000	421,000
30	1.8	4.3	5.8	106,000	251,000
20	0.7	2.4	3.1	21,000	134,000
10	0.1	1.0	1.6	8,000	51,000
2	0.0	0.0	0.2	0	8,000

[a]Percentile rank on each measure separately.

[b]Books, magazines, and newspapers.

[c]Books, magazines, newspapers, comic books, and mail.

Source: Anderson, R. C., Wilson, P. T., & Fielding, L. G. (1988). Growth in reading and how children spend their time outside of school. *Reading Research Quarterly, 23*(3), 285–303. Used with permission.

Keep in mind that those studies focused on *extra* reading that was occurring *in addition to* the time spent reading at school. Studies comparing exemplary classrooms to less effective ones found that students in the exemplary classrooms spent 90 minutes across the school day reading. In science, in social studies, math, art, and music, as well as in moments of reading for pleasure, students in these schools had eyes on print for lots of minutes. That's a volume of reading! If you add it up, children should be reading over 100 minutes per day.

>>> Why is it important in distance learning?

One concern is that in a distance learning environment, students aren't getting regular opportunities to read both for learning and for enjoyment. With live virtual sessions focused on active teaching, teachers can only hope that children are reading on their own. They may assign readings, but it is difficult for teachers to manage that when students aren't reading in front of them. If learners are not engaged in subject-related reading, their volume goes down, and their reading skills and general knowledge about the world suffers.

Reading for pleasure is another purpose for reading. In traditional face-to-face classrooms, many teachers set aside 15 or 20 minutes a day so that children can read what they choose. In some elementary schools, it may be called DEAR (Drop Everything and Read). In secondary schools, it might be called SSR (Sustained Silent Reading). In a face-to-face classroom, that works. But again, teaching at a distance makes encouraging that kind of reading a bit trickier. A daily habit of reading a lot (volume) and reading widely will move your child forward.

> **A DAILY HABIT OF READING A LOT (VOLUME) AND READING WIDELY WILL MOVE YOUR CHILD FORWARD.**

✳ Take action

One of the very best things you can do is to encourage daily reading. Don't make it a chore, but rather something to look forward to. Let your child read anything they are interested in (with your approval, of course). And follow up on the assigned readings your child's teacher has designed for them. Your child doesn't need to engage in one long marathon of reading. Break up the reading throughout the day and evening into shorter periods of time to build reading stamina. Here are additional ideas to increase children's daily reading volume:

➡ **Talk with a teacher or librarian to identify "just right" reading materials for your child.** If the texts are too complex, they will require instruction. For reading volume, the texts children read independently should be comfortable.

➡ **There are some sites that offer free electronic versions of texts for children.** A quick internet search will reveal several such as the following:

- Oxford Owl
- Storyline Online
- International Children's Digital Library
- Open Library
- Amazon's Free Kids eBooks
- Barnes & Noble Free Nook Books for Kids
- Mrs. P's Magic Library

➡️ **Read with your children.** Older children may want to read the same book as you so that they can have a shared experience with you.

➡️ **Talk with your children about what they are reading for fun.** Ask them questions about what they're reading. Don't quiz them but ask whether they are enjoying it, who they might recommend it to, or why they decided to abandon a book. (That's okay, too. Just ask them why it wasn't a good match for them.) You can also ask some generic questions, such as "What was the selection about?" Or "What has happened so far?"

➡️ **Invite your child to browse and select things to read.** Many public libraries offer digital versions of books to check out, just as you do with physical books. Look at your public library's selections and recommendations for children and adolescents. In addition, you can browse on a commercial website or on one of many useful free sites you may wish to explore, including those listed on the facing page. Choice can impact the willingness to read. Of course, there are some things that your child will need to read for school. And there will be other things that will help with the overall volume of reading. Remember, reading materials in print will also reduce your child's screen time.

➡️ **Talk to your children about what they are reading for school.** Ask questions about what they're learning and what kind of reading they're doing. If they are struggling with a reading assignment, ask them what is difficult and encourage them to communicate with the teacher. (If your child is in the primary grades, you may need to do this with them.)

➡️ **Make sure they see you reading and talking about your reading.** Parents are the very best model when it comes to building habits and dispositions about reading. Again, it can be anything, but talk about how you read every day to get information and for your own pleasure.

CHOICE CAN IMPACT THE WILLINGNESS TO READ.

🔑 Key Messages

Reading volume is an important consideration and something that you can do to support your child's learning. Remember:

➡️ Provide your child with a range of reading materials to choose from.

➡️ Plan time for reading throughout the day, including school-assigned and choice materials.

➡️ Talk with your child about what you are reading and about reading for your own enjoyment.

➡️ Model reading as a family.

THE VALUE OF READING WIDELY

What is it?

Just like a balanced diet is important for good nutrition, so is a balanced diet of types of reading. Children go through a phase where they only want to read one kind of book, and for the most part that's fine. Early readers often get hooked on a series such as *Captain Underpants, Jada Jones, Judy Moody,* or *Dog Man* and then read the entire sequence. But building knowledge also requires reading different kinds of genres. A genre is a text type, and while there are a number of ways to organize genres, the takeaway here is that knowledge-building is supported by a varied diet of books.

Why is it important?

NARRATIVE TEXTS BUILD IMAGINATION AND ENCOURAGE THE SOCIAL AND EMOTIONAL DEVELOPMENT SO ESSENTIAL TO GROWING UP.

Wide reading builds knowledge about the social, physical, and biological worlds. Each of these are important for children and adolescents. Narrative texts about the lives of real and fictional characters build imagination. Stories allow young people to encounter problems at a safe distance as they vicariously experience how a character fails and triumphs. They get to rehearse how they might confront a scary situation without having to learn by experience alone. This deepens their social and emotional development, which is so essential for growing up.

Informational texts provide children with knowledge about events and phenomena. Even in a face-to-face classroom, much of what children learn is abstract. You can't haul a volcano into a school, but informational texts about volcanos make it possible for students to learn all about them. They also foster new interests about things your child didn't even know about. We've seen kids become experts on the sinking of the *Titanic*, on deadly spiders and snakes in Australia, and about ancient African empires because they encountered an idea in a book and got hooked. Interests can become aspirations as children and adolescents learn about careers that spark their interests. And perhaps the best reason of all is one offered by the Knowledge Matters Campaign: *Knowledge is like an interest-bearing savings account: The more you know, the faster you learn* (https://knowledgematterscampaign.org/). The greater the existing knowledge, the more accelerated new learning becomes.

A challenge is that a reader may not be aware of other genres that can appeal to their interests. The genre wheel in Figure 2 is a visual map for thinking about different genres, whether digital or print.

⟫⟫ Why is it important in distance learning?

Highly effective schools ensure that their students learn about the world of information and imagination. This is crucial for reading comprehension and vocabulary, as a person's knowledge is a great predictor of how readily they're able to understand what they're reading. Equity issues also come into play here, as students who do not have access and exposure to diverse text types have a harder time developing deep levels of knowledge and therefore do not perform at grade-level standards. With much to be worried about in equitable distance learning, the gap is at risk of growing larger. Lots of reading, and reading widely, builds background knowledge and propels learning forward.

2 **GENRE WHEEL**

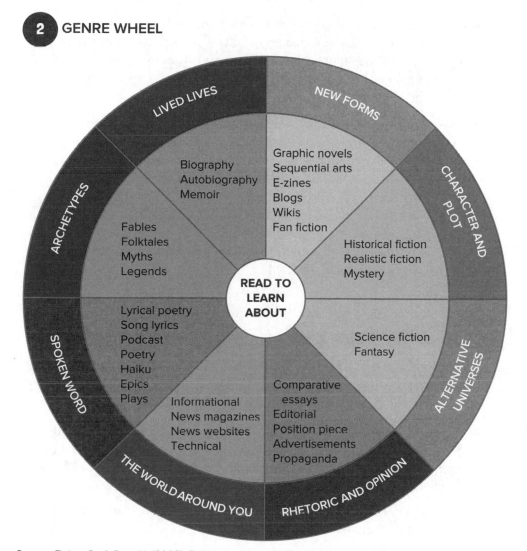

Source: Fisher, D., & Frey, N. (2009). *Background knowledge: The missing piece of the comprehension puzzle.* Portsmouth, NH: Heinemann.

 Take action

You're a great observer of what your child or adolescent is interested in. Foster her interests by pairing her up with books that align with her interests and extend them further by bridging to other genres. The good news is that you don't need to be an expert on children's and young adult literature. There are a number of organizations that develop wonderful suggested reading lists for different audiences. One well-known source is the International Library Association, which honors books each year with the Caldecott Award for illustration and the Newbery Award for writing. But there are lots of other sources you or your child can use. Here are a few of our favorites:

➜ **The International Literacy Association** publishes a list each year of the *Children's Choices Reading List* and the *Young Adults' Choices*

KNOWLEDGE IS LIKE AN INTEREST-BEARING SAVINGS ACCOUNT: THE MORE YOU KNOW, THE FASTER YOU LEARN.

Reading List, which are developed by children themselves, who read and vote on the nominees. Both lists can be found on the companion website at resources.corwin.com/DLparents.

➡️ **Guys Read** was developed by children's author Jon Scieszka, the first National Ambassador of Young People's Literature, and includes what it describes as "boy-friendly literature" across all genres. This resource can be found on the companion website at resources.corwin.com/DLparents.

➡️ **Common Sense Media** provides several book list recommendations for children and young adults, including those that are topic- or genre-specific (e.g., books about coding, anti-racist books for kids chosen by Ibram X. Kendi, memoirs, digital life, poetry, fantasy, healthy body image). Their lists provide useful information written by educators, parents, and children about the presence of sensitive topics in given texts, such as sex, drugs, violence, language, and consumerism. The lists can be found on the companion website at resources.corwin.com/DLparents.

🔑 Key Messages

Both reading volume and reading widely are important considerations that will prevent gaps in your child's knowledge and skills. Remember:

➡️ Check out your child's reading diet. Offer books on other subjects and genres that may be missing. Don't force it but rather notice it. You might even keep a log of the types of reading your child does and talk with the teacher about recommendations.

➡️ Talk with your child about both fiction and nonfiction selections. Both are important and serve different purposes.

➡️ Provide time and space for reading throughout the day.

THE VALUE OF READING ALOUD

What is it?

Young children, of course, love the laptime they get with you as you share a book. But older children also respond to read-alouds from you, and siblings who read to one another reap benefits in terms of strengthening their relationships with each other. Use read-alouds to build your child's knowledge and develop their social and emotional skills.

Why is it important?

The benefits of a family member reading aloud to a child are numerous. The academic benefits include development of vocabulary, improved listening comprehension, and achievement on reading tests. Young children get a major boost in their literacy development as they learn how stories evolve and come to understand that the print on the page carries meaning. They also learn important book handling skills such as locating the title and turning the pages. Most caregivers have been through the experience of reading to a young child who wants to hear a favorite story again and again and demands that you start over because you skipped a section! Young children often like the same story read to them before sleeping, but don't limit your read-alouds to bedtime.

The benefits of reading aloud extend to a child's social and emotional development. Young children learn about cooperation as they share a book with another person. They develop early self-regulation skills such as sitting quietly and participating in conversations. Perhaps most importantly, joint reading promotes the warmth, bonding, and close relationships that are vital in a family.

Don't underestimate the value of read-alouds for adolescents, which occur regularly in middle and high school classrooms. There is an enjoyment factor for both strong readers and those not yet making expected progress. Read-alouds can provide exposure to texts that a reluctant reader might not otherwise take on alone. As with younger readers, read-alouds can offer adolescents support in the critical areas of reading comprehension and vocabulary development.

> **JOINT READING PROMOTES THE WARMTH, BONDING, AND CLOSE RELATIONSHIPS THAT ARE VITAL IN A FAMILY.**

⟫⟫ Why is it important in distance learning?

Learning to read and reading to learn requires practice not just in instruction. Getting enough practice can be more challenging in distance learning. Importantly, anyone can be the reader when it comes to read-alouds, including your child. Given that 75 percent of children in North America grow up with at least one sibling, you may have a built-in cast ready to help. Emergent and early readers in kindergarten through third grade can practice their own developing skills by reading to a younger sibling. This has been shown to be especially effective for children who are learning the alphabet and vocabulary. Reading to younger siblings also promotes the listener's phonological awareness, which are the sounds of a language, rhyming words, and syllables. Reading specialists have been known to encourage reluctant young readers to read to the family pet because the audience is accepting.

Read-alouds are another channel for bringing books into a home routine. Older children and adolescents know how to read but benefit from shared opportunities with you. Academically, it can provide you with a way to introduce other genres to your child, including favorites from your own youth they might not otherwise pick up. Common Sense Media reminds us that read-alouds can break down barriers or bridge communication gaps between parents and their children around difficult issues they may confront such as racism, implicit biases, discrimination based on gender or religion, and violence. While they might otherwise be reluctant to talk about these directly, a book you're both reading together can create a safe space for doing so. Give one copy to your tween or teen while you read from your own copy for 15 or 20 minutes. This can be a nice wind-down ritual at the end of a busy day for both of you.

✳ Take action

You don't need to be a professional storyteller to read aloud to your child or teen. Here are a few tips for ensuring success:

➡ **Share your personality.** Your enthusiasm and willingness to display your feelings and talk about them are a great model for children. Use funny voices if it makes them laugh (even when they roll their eyes). Make sound effects, use gestures, and change your rate of reading to match what's happening in the story. All of these contribute to their growing reading comprehension.

➡ **Ask questions.** Pause occasionally to ask questions about the print (e.g., "Can you show me where the word *roar* is on this page with the lion?"), about the story (e.g., "Wait! What do you think he's going to do next now that the Captain said that?"), and about the character's emotions ("What do you see in the illustration and hear in the words that tells you how she is feeling?").

➡ **Preview the text.** It's helpful to read ahead in chapter books so you know what is coming next. It prepares you for the dramatic moments when there might need to be a pause for children to process what has occurred. Reading aloud can be a short, shared activity and does not need to be done for hours.

🔑 Key Messages

Reading aloud should be an enjoyable part of your day. It's an opportunity to share an experience with your child and strengthen bonds. Remember:

➡ Try to read aloud every day.

➡ Try to read aloud about the same time each day and build this as one of your routines—but do not limit this to a bedtime routine.

➡ Vary the texts you choose to read aloud so that you introduce your child to different types of texts as well as ideas.

➡ Consider reading aloud texts that your child might otherwise be reluctant to try.

THE VALUE OF VOCABULARY GAMES

What is it?

Vocabulary is the words of a language and their associated meanings. The more words you know, the more likely you will be to understand conversations and texts. However, simply memorizing long lists of words is not especially helpful. Use word games to increase your child's vocabulary (and perhaps your own!).

Why is it important?

Vocabulary develops across a lifetime. You know more words today than you did five years ago. And the vocabulary demand on school-age children is breathtaking. Estimates are that by the time a student enters high school, he will need to know 88,500 word families. As an example, a word family for *inform* includes *informed, information, disinformation, uninformed,* and *informant.* Many words are not a part of everyday speech (If you aren't a journalist, when was the last time you used *disinformation*?). Instead, these words are encountered primarily in written text. There's a reason why college readiness exams test vocabulary knowledge—it is a good indicator of the amount of reading applicants have done.

One way we know words is by their definition. However, knowing a definition doesn't mean you "own" a word. Knowing a word requires deepening levels of knowledge. One model describes five dimensions of vocabulary knowledge:

1. I can define the word.
2. I can use it correctly.
3. I know multiple meanings of the word.
4. I can use the word with accuracy and precision (the "just right" word).
5. I can use it in conversation and in writing.

A child's vocabulary knowledge is a solid predictor of her reading comprehension and reading achievement. And vocabulary represents a schema, or web of knowledge, that a learner possesses. The more extensive the web is, the more likely new ideas will stick. Knowing the concepts behind the word *productivity*, for instance, makes it easier to learn new ideas about *economic growth productivity* in your high schooler's economics class. In other words, vocabulary learned in one subject often shows up with slightly different meanings in other subjects. Memorizing definitions without context actually gets in the way of schema development. And college readiness exams today test vocabulary knowledge in context, not in the form of random lists of obscure words.

Word games can make vocabulary development fun while relieving some of the tedium your child might associate with the task of learning new words. There are a number of digital word games available, but you may want to reduce the amount of screen time and promote off-screen word games instead.

>>> Why is it important in distance learning?

We all make assumptions about what and how much students know. In physical school, teachers have tools to check in with students to determine if they have the conceptual knowledge and the labels (vocabulary) for those concepts. Some of these tools will translate to distance learning, but others will not. Students may have less time in an academic setting, and thus are at risk for learning fewer words. And if they are also reading less, their vocabularies may suffer.

> SIMPLY MEMORIZING LONG LISTS OF WORDS IS NOT ESPECIALLY HELPFUL.

✳ Take action

Vocabulary is one of the predictors of reading comprehension and a skill that continues to develop across the lifespan. Word acquisition and vocabulary development games can be an entertaining and low-cost way to build your child's vocabulary without her even knowing it.

> **Play board games that rely on word knowledge**. Turn family game night into a learning night. Scrabble and Scrabble Junior lead the way in this type of board game. Others that provide lots of opportunities include Balderdash, Upwords, Dabble, and Pictionary. Your child's social and emotional learning is fostered and they learn about taking turns, being a good sport, and solving problems as well.

> **Anagrams**. Use letter tiles to form a long word, then have each child see how many different words they can construct using only those letters.

> **Guess the covered word**. Write a word your child is learning on paper and cover it with a notecard. Reveal one letter at a time from left to right to see how long it takes him to figure it out. Be sure to provide a category ("It's a kind of building.") so that he is using his schema, too.

> **20 Questions**. The classic version of this verbal word game is to declare a category of animal, vegetable, or mineral and then allow the players to ask up to twenty yes/no questions about the word you're thinking of. Another variation uses the categories of a person, place, or thing (which will always yield a noun). There's a lot of deductive reasoning needed to ask the right questions to get at the answer.

MEMORIZING DEFINITIONS WITHOUT CONTEXT ACTUALLY GETS IN THE WAY OF SCHEMA DEVELOPMENT.

⚷ Key Messages

Words are everywhere and learning them is an important life skill. Remember:

> Your child's vocabulary represents her own web of knowledge. The bigger the web is, the more likely new ideas will stick.

> Make vocabulary learning fun. The whole family can get involved.

> Know the words that the teacher would like your child to learn. Include those in the games but add others.

> Be sure to take turns with your child so that you they have lots of chances to develop word puzzles to stump you!

THE VALUE OF ORAL LANGUAGE DEVELOPMENT

What is it?

Speaking with children is essential for their psychological development and is a marker for their academic development. You'll notice that we said "speaking with," not "speaking to" children. Throughout the day, we give our children directions about what to do. But we also need to engage them regularly in conversations about ideas and the world around them. These kinds of exchanges spark their mental acuity and build their vocabulary and reasoning skills, which comprise oral language development.

Why is it important?

From the moment they are born, babies soak in the language spoken around them. Long before they can speak themselves, they can detect the unique sounds, or phonemes, of their home, or native, language. By the time they are six months old, they can discern the difference between native and nonnative speech. Toddlers who are exposed to lots of language, especially the kinds of language that include asking questions and making observations about what is happening (e.g., "Your sister is helping me empty the trash. That's so helpful!") are well-prepared for early schooling. It's not so much the speech they overhear in the environment, such as when you are speaking to another adult, or from a television playing in the background, but rather speech that is directed at the child.

These benefits continue throughout childhood and adolescence. Sometimes as parents we wonder whether what we say to older children and teenagers is making a difference. Let us assure you—it makes all the difference. Your conversations with them about their interests and their worries are invaluable in helping them to form schemas for how they make decisions and address problems. When you share how you approach a problem, you are modeling the kind of reasoning that is invaluable to them in their academic studies and in life.

>>> Why is it important in distance learning?

Household routines have become a lot more complicated during the pandemic. Adults may be working from inside the home or working outside the home using far more elaborate routines than usual to stay safe and healthy. Your children are engaged in various distance learning schedules that may require the skills of a professional juggler to arrange physical spaces and allot devices. In the face of these demands, it is understandable that time for quality conversation suffers.

In face-to-face classrooms, students are accustomed to conversations with teachers, friends, and classmates throughout the day. But in distance learning, the opportunities to engage in these conversations is more limited. Yet the need for young people to be active participants in conversations continues, and your household becomes an even more important hub for communication that matters.

✳ Take action

In addition to the conversations you have throughout the day with your child, consider adding a conversational routine that meets the social and emotional needs of your child. Here are a few to consider:

➡ **Apples and onions.** Each person in the family names something they saw or experienced that was a positive (apple) and one thing that was more challenging (onion). Checking in like this helps all the members of the household stay abreast of each other's lives and provide a springboard for solving problems together.

➡ **Pose a question of the day.** Post a thought-provoking question on the refrigerator or family bulletin board each morning and tell your child you'll check in later in the day. Here are ten questions to get you started:

1. What do people like about you?

2. What is something you would like for me to do more often?

3. What is your favorite day of the week?

4. What is your first memory as a little kid?

5. If you could only eat four things for the rest of your life, what would they be?

6. If you were a professional wrestler, what would your entrance song be?

7. If you could relive one day of your life, which day would you choose?

8. What would you wait in a long line for?

9. What is your favorite saying or poem?

10. When you're an adult, what stories do you think children will ask you to tell?

➡ **Song of the day.** Each member of the family takes turns choosing a song of the day to be played and explains why they chose the song.

➡ **Family photo of the week.** Post a photograph of a family event that occurred in the past and ask your child what he remembers from that day, or about the people in the photograph. Old family photograph albums are another great source for starting conversations about memories.

🔑 Key Messages

For most children, their listening comprehension cannot exceed their reading comprehension. Building oral language skills will pay dividends in reading as well. Remember:

➡️ Engage in conversations with your child. Ask them about their experiences and ideas.

➡️ Create a language rich environment in your home filled with talk.

➡️ Provide your child opportunities to talk with others. Screen time for this has actually been shown to be effective in developing literacy skills.

THE VALUE OF FOUNDATIONAL READING SKILLS: PHONEMIC AWARENESS

What is it?

Phonemes are the smallest units of sound in a language. They allow you, for instance, to hear the difference between *cup* and *cups,* because your brain can discern the /s/ sound. Young children who are learning to read use their phonemic awareness skills to figure out the letters and words in print. Typically, older students have developed phonemic awareness so depending on the age of your child and their current reading performance, this may or may not be a priority.

Why is it important?

Have you had the experience of attempting to speak in a language you were not conversant in? You may have tried to replicate a word or phrase a native speaker told you, but when you repeated it, they said, "No, that's not quite right" and said it again more slowly. Despite your attempts, you didn't get the hang of it, even as you swore you were pronouncing the words exactly the same way. You may have confronted your own lack of phonemic awareness in that language.

Each human language has a range of sounds, or phonemes, that make speech understandable to other speakers. English has 44 phonemes, Spanish has 24, and !Xóõ (pronounced /kō/ in English), a Botswanan language, has 112 phonemes. Infants learn the phonemes of a language and continue to develop this throughout the first years of school. Primary teachers promote the development of phonemic awareness with their students because it is critical in their reading development.

A child's growing phonemic awareness makes it possible for them to hear the pauses between words, to detect rhyming words, and to hear the difference between similar sounding words like *weather* and *wetter.* (When Nancy's daughter was small, she would call a *canopy bed* a *panicky bed.*) Teachers play games that involve clapping to the sounds in a word and using chants, songs, and poems. Later stages of phonemic awareness include the following:

➡️ Blending sounds and splitting syllables, such as being able to listen to the sounds of /m/ and /āl/ to say *mail*; recognizing that *mailbox* consists of two syllable sounds

➡️ Segmenting sounds, which is the opposite of blending sounds; a child at this stage can take apart the sounds in a spoken word (e.g., *flew* has two phonemes: /fl/ and /oo/).

➡️ Manipulating sounds by deleting, substituting, adding, and reversing phonemes; an example of reversing phonemes is to hear the word *let* and saying it backward as *tell*.

TALK WITH YOUR CHILD'S TEACHER ABOUT HOW HE OR SHE IS ASSESSING PHONEMIC AWARENESS.

Measurement of a child's phonemic awareness skills can be more challenging in a distance learning environment. Talk with your child's teacher about how he or she is assessing phonemic awareness. Some schools are experiencing success in assessing these skills by asking the parent, if so inclined, to record themselves assessing their child and then submitting it to the teacher for analysis and to design instruction. One of the most widely used tools is called the Yopp-Singer Test of Phoneme Segmentation. It is administered orally and takes less than ten minutes to complete. We have included it in Figure 3 if you are interested in using it. We have included the answer key in Figure 4.

It is important to note that if your child is older and has mastered phonemic awareness, there is no reason to continue to promote it from an educational sense. However, if your child is learning a subsequent language to complement his native language(s), then he is also moving through similar stages of development of his phonemic awareness of the new language.

⟫⟫ Why is it important in distance learning?

Emergent readers need lots of opportunities to play with the sounds of language. Primary grade teachers will prioritize these opportunities in a distance learning environment. If you overhear your child's teacher singing songs, using poems for rhyming, and playing other word games, recognize that this is exactly why they are doing so. Ask your child's teacher to provide examples of songs and word games you can use at home to reinforce learning of phonemic awareness.

✳️ Take action

Child developmental psychologist Jean Piaget famously said that play is the work of children, and word games that promote the sounds of language are well worth the investment of time for your young reader. Here are ideas for how to promote phonemic awareness, depending on your child's developmental stage:

➡️ **Clap the words or syllables.** Challenge your child to make a sentence with a fixed number of words. For instance, you might ask, "Can you call everyone to dinner and say it in four words?" Rehearse her sentence and clap it with her before she calls everyone. "Dinner's ready! Please come!"

➡️ *Sing songs and chants that capitalize on word play.* Nursery rhymes like "1, 2, Buckle My Shoe," songs like "Apples and Bananas," and jump rope chants such as "Miss Mary Mack" are just a few of many examples you might use. Undoubtedly you have your own favorites, so please use them.

➡️ *Read picture books that encourage word play interactions.* There are many, of course, but a few of our favorites include *Joseph Had a Little Overcoat* by Sims Tayback, *Brown Bear, Brown Bear* by Eric Carle, *A Crash of Rhinos* by Greg Danylyshyn, and *The Book with No Pictures* by B. J. Novak.

> **IF YOUR CHILD IS OLDER AND HAS MASTERED PHONEMIC AWARENESS, THERE IS NO REASON TO CONTINUE TO PROMOTE IT.**

3 YOPP-SINGER TEST OF PHONEME SEGMENTATION

Name: _____ Date: _____

Score (number correct): _____

Directions: Today we're going to play a word game. I'm going to say a word and I want you to break the word apart. You are going to tell me each sound in the word in order. For example, if I say "old," you should say "/o/ - /l/ - /d/."

(Administrator: Be sure to say the sounds, not the letters, in the word.) Let's try a few together.

Practice items: *(Assist the child in segmenting these items as necessary.)* ride, go, man

Test items: *(Circle those items that the student correctly segments; incorrect responses may be recorded on the blank line following the item.)*

1.	dog	_____	12.	lay	_____
2.	keep	_____	13.	race	_____
3.	fine	_____	14.	zoo	_____
4.	no	_____	15.	three	_____
5.	she	_____	16.	job	_____
6.	wave	_____	17.	in	_____
7.	grew	_____	18.	ice	_____
8.	that	_____	19.	at	_____
9.	red	_____	20.	top	_____
10.	me	_____	21.	by	_____
11.	sat	_____	22.	do	_____

Source: Yopp, H. K. (1995). A test for assessing phonemic awareness in young children. *The Reading Teacher, 49,* 20–29. Used with permission.

ANSWER KEY FOR YOPP-SINGER TEST OF PHONEME SEGMENTATION

Name: _____ Date: _____

Score (number correct): _____

Directions: Today we're going to play a word game. I'm going to say a word and I want you to break the word apart. You are going to tell me each sound in the word in order. For example, if I say "old," you should say "/o/ - /l/ - /d/."

(Administrator: Be sure to say the sounds, not the letters, in the word.) Let's try a few together.

Practice items: *(Assist the child in segmenting these items as necessary.)* ride, go, man

Test items: *(Circle those items that the student correctly segments; incorrect responses may be recorded on the blank line following the item.)*

1.	dog	/d/ - /o/ - /g/	12.	lay	/l/ - /a/
2.	keep	/k/ - /e/ - /p/	13.	race	/r/ - /a/ - /s/
3.	fine	/f/ - /i/ - /n/	14.	zoo	/z/ - /oo/
4.	no	/n/ - /o/	15.	three	/th/ - /r/ - /e/
5.	she	/sh/ - /e/	16.	job	/j/ - /o/ - /b/
6.	wave	/w/ - /a/ - /v/	17.	in	/i/ - /n/
7.	grew	/g/- /r/ - /oo/	18.	ice	/i/ - /s/
8.	that	/th/- /a/ - /t/	19.	at	/a/ - /t/
9.	red	/r/- /e/ - /d/	20.	top	/t/- /o/ - /p/
10.	me	/m/- /e/	21.	by	/b/ - /i/
11.	sat	/s/ - /a/- /t/	22.	do	/d/- /oo/

Source: Yopp, H. K. (1995). A test for assessing phonemic awareness in young children. *The Reading Teacher, 49*, 20–29. Used with permission.

 Key Messages

Children need to learn the sounds used in a language to develop both speaking and reading skills. Remember:

➜ Understanding the sounds of the language starts as soon as babies are born.

➜ Play with the sounds of language often.

➜ Singing and rhyming help develop phonemic awareness.

➜ There are games for blending, substituting, and deleting sounds in spoken words that provide practice.

THE VALUE OF FOUNDATIONAL READING SKILLS: ALPHABETICS AND PHONICS

What is it?

Many languages, including English, use an alphabet system to represent the sounds of the language. Young children master the alphabet as a part of their journey to reading. Alphabetics include the names of the letters and their associated sounds, which serves as the foundation for phonics (combining sounds and letters into words). Alphabetic knowledge aids readers in word recognition and decoding.

Why is it important?

Many children begin to learn letters before they have entered school. Early letter recognition often begins with recognizing the letters in their first names. But keep in mind that there aren't twenty-six letters in the English alphabet, but rather fifty-two when you count both uppercase and lowercase representations. Now add a few more, as depending on the font, lowercase letters might be represented as *a* or *ɑ* and *g* or **g**. To a young child, these look like random squiggles on a page. Over time and with practice, both the letter shapes and the letter sounds converge. Decoding, which is pronouncing words accurately, is dependent in part on a child's easy recognition of letters and sounds. Teachers teach phonics, or breaking the code, to accomplish this.

You might recall from your own schooling that there was a "letter of the week" and that your class progressed from the letter *A* in the first week to the letter *Z* in the twenty-sixth week. That formula is not used anymore, as there is greater understanding that some letters are easier than others to learn. For example, the uppercase letters *A, B, X,* and *O* are known by most four-year-olds. Letter sounds that sound like their name (*s, m,* and *z*) are among the first mastered by four-year-olds. Among the last to be mastered in terms of naming the letter and its corresponding sounds are *y, w, c, i, o,* and *e*. Keep in mind that these letters have more than one sound. Therefore, teaching alphabetic principles means that more time is dedicated to those harder-to-learn skills.

We've included an alphabet knowledge sheet to use with your child if you would like to assess what they know and don't know in Figure 5. We have also included a recording sheet so you can track their growing alphabetics knowledge. It is in Figure 6, and a downloadable copy is also available at resources.corwin.com/DLparents. Young children also like to write letters and words they know, especially their names. Every primary teacher is grateful if you have taught your child how to write their name using the correct combination of upper and lowercase letters.

>>> Why is it important in distance learning?

Learning the letters and sounds takes lots of instruction, practice, and exposure, and as we have said previously, time is a precious commodity in distance learning.

Undoubtedly, teachers in the primary grades and those who teach students with disabilities will provide direct and systematic instruction in alphabetics and phonics. But, some of your child's asynchronous learning needs to be dedicated to practicing these skills. We hope that in addition to worksheets, there are fun activities provided that engage your child.

✳ Take action

Mastering the alphabet and its sounds is an essential skill for emergent readers and writers. In addition to activities promoted by your child's teacher, consider using some of these approaches:

→ **Find out which letters and sound combinations the teacher is teaching.** Practice those with your child. You may print off decodable texts from a site such as The Text Project for practice. You can also create flashcards with the patterns the teacher is teaching. For example, if your child is learning the -*op* ending, you can have a card with *op* written on it and then several options for letters that could start a word (e.g., *h*, *l*, *st*, *t*, and *fl*). The link to The Text Project can be found on the companion website at resources.corwin.com/DLparents.

→ **Make whole-body letter shapes.** Remember the dance routine that accompanied the chorus of the Village People song, "YMCA"? Join your child in making body shapes into letters. It is fun, but it is also a great way to help them internalize the letter shapes. Unlike the dance routine, you don't need to confine yourself to only using arms. These gross-motor movements are exercise for your child and can aid in burning off some extra energy.

→ **Use creative materials to write and rehearse letters.** Make letters from pipe cleaners, write them in chalk on the sidewalk, and paint with water on paper (no need for paint—the water alone will leave a visible shape). Another novel way is to fill a cake pan with sand or rice and let the child trace letters in the material. Be sure to reinforce the sounds of the letters and corresponding representative words (e.g., "*L* is for *love* and makes the /l/ sound.").

→ **Make the most of alphabet books.** There are countless alphabet books available in for every imaginable theme. Use your child's interests to guide alphabet book choices. Whether the theme is construction vehicles, dinosaurs, or hip-hop, there's an alphabet book for him or her. A bonus is that themed alphabet books expand your child's vocabulary and schema about a concept.

5 STUDENT FORM FOR LETTER IDENTIFICATION

O	W	E	X
S	A	G	D
H	K	P	J
C	N	U	V
Y	R	B	I
Q	L	F	M
Z	T		

o	w	e	x
s	a	g	d
h	k	p	j
c	n	u	v
y	r	b	i
q	l	f	m
z	t	a	g

6 RECORDING FORM FOR LETTER IDENTIFICATION

Name: _____ Date: _____

Teacher: _____

Letter	Correct	Incorrect	Letter	Correct	Incorrect
O			o		
W			w		
E			e		
X			x		
S			s		
A			a		
G			g		
D			d		
H			h		
K			k		

(Continued)

(Continued)

Letter	Correct	Incorrect	Letter	Correct	Incorrect
P			p		
J			j		
C			c		
N			n		
U			u		
V			v		
Y			y		
R			r		
B			b		
I			i		
Q			q		
L			l		
F			f		
M			m		
Z			z		
T			t		
			a		
			g		
Total uppercase	/26	/26	Total lowercase	/28	/28

Code of scoring: Correct = ✓
    Incorrect = record student response

Source: Fisher, D., Frey, N., & Hattie, J. (2017). *Teaching literacy in the visible learning classroom, grades K–5.* Corwin.

online resources | Available for download at **resources.corwin.com/DLparents**

🔑 Key Messages

Developing an understanding of relationship between sounds and symbols takes time, and both instruction and practice are necessary. Remember:

➡ Practice makes learning permanent.

➡ Know what the teacher is teaching and reinforce that.

➡ Make learning alphabetics and phonics fun.

THE VALUE OF FOUNDATIONAL READING SKILLS: FLUENCY

What is it?

Oral reading fluency is the ability to read accurately and smoothly aloud. Fluency is a foundational skill; readers with oral reading fluency are able to devote more attention to meaning because they are accurately decoding and recognizing words. Readers in Grades 1 through 8 are working toward improving their fluency using grade-level text. Fluency is more than the rate, or speed that you read. It's also the way it is read, called *prosody,* which includes tone, emphasis, pauses, and inflections.

FLUENCY IS MORE THAN THE RATE, OR SPEED THAT YOU READ. IT'S ALSO THE WAY IT IS READ, WHICH IS CALLED PROSODY.

Why is it important?

During elementary school, readers are braiding together their ability to recognize words and to comprehend what they read. For early readers, these two skills are somewhat separate from one another and both take quite a bit of effort. But as they get better at recognizing words, some of that attention can go "underground" so to speak. As their decoding becomes more subconscious, readers can use more of their attention to concentrate on the meaning of what they are reading. This process, called *automaticity*, contributes to a child's ability to read for understanding. Reading fluency, which is a measure of accuracy and rate, continues to evolve through sixth grade for readers making expected progress.

Measures of reading fluency are designed in such a way that they continually challenge students. As the rate of fluency increases, so too does the complexity of the text your child is expected to be able to read. It would be expected that a fourth grader could read a first-grade text accurately and at an acceptable rate, but that doesn't actually tell you if the child can read fourth-grade texts fluently. It would be like continuing to ride a bicycle with training wheels long after that support was no longer needed. Thus, the goal is for children to read grade-level texts with good fluency. If you are interested in knowing about your child's fluency, we have included a chart of grade-level expectations at the beginning, middle, and end of the school year. Oral reading fluency in first grade is not measured until the middle of the school year.

>>> Why is it important in distance learning?

Reading fluency is fostered by doing lots of reading, not just doing fluency exercises. Maintaining a volume of reading is necessary for students to make continual progress. The assigned reading your child completes asynchronously contributes to his subject knowledge and in the process makes him an increasingly fluent reader. Your child might also be engaged in reading activities with peers designed to boost fluency. For instance, she might be doing paired reading. This strategy requires each child to read the same passage silently to familiarize themselves with the text, and to then take turns reading it aloud to one another. Your child's teacher may construct some lessons so that repeated reading occurs, as when he asks questions about a short piece of text that requires the reader to return to the text and look for evidence (e.g., "What does the author say about the mood of the character?"). In addition to building comprehension, techniques like this build reading fluency.

READING FLUENCY IS FOSTERED BY DOING LOTS OF READING, NOT JUST DOING FLUENCY EXERCISES.

✳ Take action

Fluent reading is foundational for reading growth. Children need lots of opportunities to read, and to read things more than one time. It isn't uncommon for a child to lament, "But I read that already!" Help your child build fluency by engaging in repeated reading that is fun and purposeful. Here are a few ideas:

➡ **Read-alongs.** The research world calls this the neurologic impress method. You read aloud as your child reads aloud, but you try to read at a slightly faster pace than your child so that this impresses in their minds. You also vary the speed, based on the text, and use natural pauses and inflections appropriate for the text. Your child will begin to speed up to keep pace with you. And your child will notice the ways that you use your voice to make it sound more like talking and less like a robot. After the reading, you talk about what the text said to ensure that they understood the text.

➡ **Dialogue drama.** When reading aloud with your child, take advantage of sections of dialogue between characters to do some repeated reading. Each of you assumes the identity of one of the characters and uses expression to make them come to life. You can remind your child to "make it sound like talking" by using the correct tone and inflection. The goal is not to memorize the dialogue, but to build more fluent reading. In fact, your child should be keeping an eye on the text. See if you can't encourage them to read it again, which promotes further repeated reading.

➡ **Radio plays.** There are lots of scripts of old radio plays available on the internet, and they lend themselves beautifully to a technique called *readers theater*. These radio plays do not require props, costumes, or staging. Instead, each performer reads directly from the script. There are numerous readers theater scripts for children ages 8 to 15 online, and some can be found on the companion website at resources .corwin.com/DLparents. Older children might like to perform *5 Minute Mysteries*, a radio show from the 1940s where the goal is to figure out who committed the crime during the commercial break. Organize family members and cast roles for each. Make sure they have rehearsal time (repeated reading) and remind them that they will always read from the script. No memorizing! Episodes of *5 Minute Mysteries* can be found on the companion website at resources.corwin.com/DLparents.

➡ **Encourage rereading favorite books.** Fluency doesn't come from constantly reading new material—children need opportunities to read familiar ones, too. Talk about favorite books that you return to even though you have read them before. If there are younger siblings in the house, encourage your child to read old favorites to the younger ones.

🔑 Key Messages

Fluency is another predictor of reading comprehension. When a child reads too slowly and focuses on sounding out each word, he is not likely to retain what he read. Remember:

➡ Fluency is more than speed; it's also the way reading sounds.

➡ Practice fluency aloud and know that the inner voice will develop as children read silently.

➡ Look at the norms, or averages, from research to know if you need to spend more time on this (see Figure 7). If your child is well below these norms, you may want to talk with the teacher about additional ways to increase fluency.

7 **ORAL READING FLUENCY NORMS**

Grade	Fall WCPM*	Winter WCPM*	Spring WCPM*
1		29	60
2	50	84	100
3	83	97	112
4	94	120	133
5	121	133	146
6	132	145	146

*WCPM = Words Correct Per Minute

Source: Adapted from Hasbrouck, J., & Tindal, G. (2017). *An update to compiled ORF norms* (Technical Report No. 1702). Eugene: Behavioral Research and Teaching, University of Oregon.

THE VALUE OF WRITING ACROSS THE DAY

What is it?

In addition to the writing that students are required to do during their school day, there are many writing tasks that arise organically over the course of your everyday life with your children. Your household offers an endless array of writing opportunities. When you notice those opportunities, pause, and take advantage of them. Your child will reap the benefits. After all, the best kind of writing is fueled by authentic purposes and a clear intended audience.

Why is it important?

People compose for three main purposes: to convey real or imagined experiences, to provide information, and to share opinions and arguments about an issue. But getting these ideas down requires handwriting or typing skills, spelling, grammar, and conventions such as using capital letters and punctuation in the right places. And that's before we even consider forming and organizing ideas, understanding what the purpose is for your writing, and knowing who your audience is. In other words, children and adolescents have to coordinate a lot of different skills in order to compose a meaningful message.

THE BEST KIND OF WRITING IS FUELED BY AUTHENTIC PURPOSES AND A CLEAR INTENDED AUDIENCE.

Before we go any further, it is important to know that we are not encouraging you to assign your child a research paper or an essay. Those are school-based writing tasks that should come from your child's teacher. But writing and composition can happen in authentic and naturalistic ways. First, note how often you write throughout the day. In addition to your professional obligations, you make lists, send text messages to friends, jot down notes to yourself (often labeled "Do not forget!"), write a quick math calculation to figure out the sales tax on an item, and send thank-you notes. Perhaps you even journal, or you keep a sleep, exercise, or food diary to track a habit you'd like to improve. No one is insisting that you write; you do so because it is functional and efficient. Consider this thought—humans are the only species that can store information outside of their bodies. Writing is what makes this possible.

⟫⟫ Why does it matter in distance learning?

Just like pretty much anything that we want to get better at, writing requires practice. There is growing evidence that writing by hand benefits young children in terms of their reading. If your child is learning from a distance, this is something you'll want to ensure is happening at home. If your child is young, keep lots of thick pencils, crayons, and scissors around so she can develop the fine motor skills she needs to write legibly, and encourage her to read you what she wrote. Older children should be encouraged to write things down on paper and not just on their smartphone to maintain their handwriting skills.

Fluent writing is aided by the ability to spell correctly. Very young children move through stages of early writing that include a lot of transitional and temporary spellings. You don't need to (and you actually shouldn't try to) "fix" everything, especially when it is not yet useful from a developmental perspective. In other words, if the teacher hasn't taught it yet, try not to worry about it. Composing provides writers with the practice needed to apply grammar rules correctly. You might recall some dreary grammar exercises in your own schooling. Writing lifts those experiences into more practical applications. When you spot a grammatical error with an older writer, rather than correct it, simply ask him to read the sentences aloud and ask whether that sounds right to him. Often that is enough to get him moving again.

 Take action

Notice the authentic purposes for writing that naturally and spontaneously occur in your household and harness those as opportunities for your children to practice. None of these writing suggestions are meant to be onerous to either your children or you. Talk about how their writing is helping the family and reinforce the aspect of pleasure that writing can bring. Here are some ways to bring writing into your home:

➡ **Set up a post office for young children.** Set up a cardboard mail sorter that has cubbies in it (available at most office supply stores) and stock it with paper, envelopes, writing instruments, and stamps (not real ones—adhesive stickers do the trick). You might even have an ink stamper to "cancel" the stamp. Label some of the cubbies with the names of each family member and encourage everyone to leave "mail" in the form of notes for one another.

➡ **Enlist list makers.** Whether they are related to groceries, errands, or general to-dos, households run on lists to catalog the many things needed to keep everyone organized. Rather than make the lists yourself, ask your child to make the list for you. You can dictate what needs to go on the list but have her write it for you. Food preparation time is a great time of the day to dictate a list while you cook.

➡ **Buy a diary or journal for each child.** Without question, this period of time will be something your children will talk about for the rest of their lives. Encourage them to write and draw daily in a journal about current events, their hopes and fears, and anything else that inspires them. Remind them to date the entry so they have a record of their younger selves. They don't need to share this with anyone if they don't want to. However, you may discover that the cathartic act of writing encourages them to talk with you about their lives and concerns, which is crucial for their mental well-being.

➡ **Keep a growing list of gratitudes.** Post a scroll, large piece of paper, or a family chalkboard with the heading, "What are you grateful for?" Each day ask each member of the household to add one thing they are grateful for. When the list is full, take a photograph of it and start over. You might continue with this question or add a different one. Let them see how the list grows while reminding them about the positives they are experiencing.

➡ **Bring back thank-you notes.** Hall of Fame football quarterback Peyton Manning is famous for writing thank-you notes to colleagues, friends, and acquaintances, and YouTube is filled with videos of those who have received them. Manning states that he learned this from his mother, who required her children to write thank-you notes. It's a habit that stuck for Manning, and the research on writing notes of gratitude demonstrates that the greatest benefit is the writer's mental health and well-being. The art of handwritten correspondence was nearly gone, but with physical distancing has come the desire to connect with those we don't get to see regularly. Ask each of your children to write one thank-you note a week to a family member, friend, first responder, or anyone who is deserving of thanks.

> WE ARE NOT ENCOURAGING YOU TO ASSIGN YOUR CHILD A RESEARCH PAPER OR AN ESSAY.

 **Key Messages**

Humans write for many reasons. Nearly every writer can read but not all readers can write. And writing can become a natural part of the day for children. Remember:

➡ Provide materials for your child to write: a notebook and writing tools at least.

➡ Talk with your child about writing. Ask them to share their writing. Perhaps you even create an "author's chair" and dedicate time for people sitting in the chair to share their writing.

➡ Model writing in a variety of ways for your children to see that it is natural and useful.

THE VALUE OF SCAFFOLDED WRITING EXPERIENCES

What is it?

If you are looking for ways to take a more active role in supporting your child's writing, scaffolded writing activities are for you. These are techniques for fostering your child's use of grammar, conventions, and composition in writing. These routines are designed to boost the daily output of writing and contribute to increased writing fluency.

Why is it important?

A common criticism of writing instruction is that the emphasis is often on *causing* writing to occur, rather than on providing instruction on writing skills. Writing instruction requires more than just providing a prompt to "write about a time when you . . ." In fact, many teachers will tell you that when faced with a prompt, a reluctant writer often has trouble getting started and instead says "I'm thinking." However, in truth there's no action and the writer has trouble leaving the starting line. Scaffolded writing offers a way to focus on different aspects of writing and in some cases to get the child started. These routines don't take a lot of time and can easily complement instruction your child's teacher is providing.

Scaffolding is a common instructional technique designed to bridge what a learner knows with what a learner does not know *yet*. Think of the scaffolding on the outside of a building as a metaphor for this technique. A scaffolding structure extends the reach of the worker, and it is taken down when the work is completed. Scaffolded instruction is also temporary and is intended to extend the learning of students by reaching for something that they might not otherwise be able to get to on their own.

And once they have mastered a concept or a skill, they don't need the scaffolding any longer. Scaffolding is a teaching tool used in every subject area from pre-K to graduate programs.

》》》 Why is it important in distance learning?

Elementary and secondary students who are finding writing to be challenging can benefit from additional opportunities to compose. As with reading, the volume of writing produced matters. Some of the writing skills taught in school, such as editing and revising, can't even happen unless there is something to work with. These scaffolded writing techniques are intended to boost the volume of writing while building vocabulary skills and idea formation.

✳ Take action

Here are four scaffolded writing techniques that build writing skills and can spark children's imaginations when a writing assignment seems too daunting to begin:

➡ **Language experience approach.** This technique was developed decades ago for a literacy project for indigenous women in South America. The idea is to take some dictation down as a person tells a story, then use what has been written as a source for reading practice. It has been widely adapted for young children, who draw a picture and then tell a story to an adult who writes down their words for them. You can use this approach with your child to get them started on a writing assignment. Discuss the prompt with them and write down key ideas they verbalize. Take a look at these two or three sentences together to hone them and have your child use these sentences in their writing.

➡ **Interactive writing.** Similarly, discuss the topic of the writing assignment, this time agreeing on what an opening paragraph might include. Once the message has been jointly composed orally, have your child write it out. Your job is to repeat the agreed message (you might want to jot this down on note paper). As she writes, ask her to consider in advance letters that should be capitalized, what punctuation is needed, and how each word is spelled.

➡ **Generative sentences.** Most school writing assignments involve a specific topic of study. Take the vocabulary assigned for the unit and use these words as a way to scaffold short writing passages. The generative sentences technique requires that you place limits on the sentence, both in the length of the sentence and the position of the word. As an example, perhaps a vocabulary word associated with a unit on space is *planet*. Give your child conditions for both: "Write a sentence that uses the word *planet* in the third position in a sentence that is at least seven words long." Now they are thinking simultaneously about the definition of the word and the grammar that they have to use in order to create a sentence that makes sense. They might write, "The closest *planet* to the Sun is Mercury." Repeat this exercise with four or five other vocabulary terms that they will probably use in the writing assignment, varying the position of the word each time and the length of the sentence. In a matter of a few minutes, they have already written several sentences. Now ask them to choose one of the sentences as a topic sentence for a paragraph. They can select others that are useful, too. What they have accomplished is pretty impressive, as they went from the word level, to the sentence level, to the paragraph level in a matter of minutes.

→ **Power writing.** This last technique is about building writing fluency and it works well with elementary as well as secondary students. It is a timed writing exercise and takes less than five minutes to complete. The goal here is to achieve your personal best each day by writing as much as you can, as well as you can, for one minute. It can help to give them a word for inspiration, although it is not necessary for them to use the word or even stick to that topic. Then start the clock.

Repeat this for a total of three times, counting the number of words written each time (1 minute). Typically, the number will increase by the third time because their writing fluency is increasing. Ask them to graph their personal best results for the day in order to keep a record of how their writing fluency is increasing over time. Then ask your child or teen to review what they have written. They don't need to correct errors, just circle where they have occurred. This gives you a sense of what they are noticing and what they have missed. It can be helpful to keep all the power writing your child accomplishes in a single notebook, as it can be a source for later inspiration when they say that they are not sure what they want to write about for an assignment.

Key Messages

This topic is more instructional. As such, it's more invitational. If you have the time, or your child has the need, you may want to engage in scaffolded writing lessons. Remember:

➡ Scaffolding is temporary and should be removed as the child experiences success.

➡ It's about approximations of success, not perfect writing.

➡ Power writing can be useful in building stamina and can provide you with ideas about the strengths and needs in terms of your child's writing.

THE VALUE OF MATHEMATICS ACROSS THE DAY

What is it?

As with reading and writing, there are chances throughout the day for your child to use mathematics skills for authentic purposes. Take advantage of opportunities to get your child practicing these skills to keep them fresh. With your influence, they can gain a new appreciation for the importance of math in everyday life.

Why is it important?

REL Northwest, an educational laboratory operated by the U.S. Department of Education, offers two pieces of advice for families about mathematics:

1. Help your child develop a positive mindset about mathematics. Don't tell them, "I'm not a math person" or "I hated math class in school," as it can reinforce a false belief that they can't do math either.

2. Teach children how mathematics is visible in the world. You can view their short video for families titled "Two Strategies to Help Your Child Learn to Love Math" on the companion website at resources.corwin.com/DLparents.

>>> Why is it important in distance learning?

We work with a mathematics teacher who likes to remind his students that "mastery requires maintenance." We couldn't agree more. Mathematics skills can get stale pretty quickly when there isn't much call for practicing. Worksheets and online games can provide some practice, but the mathematics used by your family every day provides a whole new level of relevance. In answer to the question, "Why do I have to learn this?" (usually said with a whiny voice) you can amplify the relevance by showing them just how useful it is.

Relevance makes learning happen more quickly. When a learner understands *why* she is learning a concept or skill, the pace of learning accelerates. In other words, the child learns faster because she sees the value in it. We know that when learning is made more responsive and culturally relevant, the learning quickens. And this is exactly the place where families are so strong because you have the insight and wisdom to see how mathematics is utilized in your household and community. You have tremendous influence on your child's perceptions of what is valued. When you talk about the everyday mathematics you use, your child gains a deeper appreciation of the subject.

RELEVANCE MAKES LEARNING HAPPEN MORE QUICKLY.

✳ Take action

Mathematics is sometimes incorrectly perceived as something they only use during a designated time during the school day. When you discuss math from a family perspective, you help them see its practical benefits and its relevance to their lives. With this in mind, here are some ideas for how you can do so.

➡ **Make up word problems on your walks.** If your child is young, point out places at home or in the neighborhood where you see numerals, such as on mailboxes and street signs. Older children can keep track of how many items they see on the walk (e.g., dogs, houses of worship, lampposts, or neon signs). Children who are learning shapes can play a version of I Spy by naming and counting the number of triangles they see, or cubes, or octagons (think stop signs). Children in the upper grades can formulate words problems based on what they see. For example, a store with posted hours becomes a word problem: How many hours will they be open this week?

➡️ **Reinforce telling time and elapsed time.** We are continually surprised at how many teens don't know how to tell time on analog dial clocks. They have become so accustomed to looking at digital time on phones, appliances, and cars that they don't recognize how a dial clock face represents 12:15. This may seem like a small thing but that also means that they don't understand when we say, "It's a quarter past 12." Seriously, blank looks. If you have an analog clock or watch, get it out and see if your teen can tell the time. If he can, it's all good. But if he can't, ask him questions about the time as it relates to family events. It only takes a bit of practice before he'll get the hang of it. Elapsed time can be challenging for younger children, especially those who do not regularly use public transportation and don't have experience with reading timetables. Follow up time questions they ask with a question of your own about how much time will need to go by before the next event occurs (e.g., "It's 6:18 now and dinner will be about 7:00. So how much time will you need to wait?").

➡️ **Show your children how you use mathematics in your life.** Whether you are refilling the gas tank of your car, calculating a bill, or planning when to leave the house so you can arrive at work on time, you're using math. Simply drawing attention to presence of math in your life can reinforce its relevance.

➡️ **Expose your child to the unique contributions of various cultures to mathematics.** The concept of zero was independently devised thousands of years ago in Mesopotamia and by the Mayans. India spread the concept of zero in the 5th century and expanded it to Cambodia and Vietnam. Islamic cultures were using zero by the 8th century. Western Europe was late to the game—zero did not appear until the 12th century. Ask your child to investigate mathematicians and math contributions. Introduce them to

- Mayan math
- Math from China
- Islamic math and science contributions

Links to resources on these math contributions can be found on the companion website at resources.corwin.com/DLparents.

 ## Key Messages

Mathematics is sometimes incorrectly perceived as something they only use during a designated time during the school day. When you discuss math from a family perspective, you help them see its practical benefits and its relevance to their lives. Remember:

➡️ Reinforce math concepts your child is learning by pointing out how you use the same skills.

➡ Look for opportunities to get your child thinking mathematically at home and in the community.

➡ Foster cultural relevance by asking your child to investigate contributions to mathematics in your heritage culture and others.

THE VALUE OF SUPPLEMENTAL MATHEMATICS INSTRUCTION

What is it?

Perhaps you are interested in having your child participate in supplemental mathematics instruction. It may be due to their interest in the subject, or because you would like them to have more practice beyond regular school instruction. Free online mathematics lessons through the Khan Academy can be a useful site for your child.

Why is it important?

We rarely profile a specific organization at length, but we must admit that we have been fans and users of Khan Academy for many years. Khan Academy was the brainchild of Salman Khan, who created the nonprofit in 2009 after he started posting videos of tutorials he devised for his cousins on YouTube. Teachers and students responded to the engaging style of the videos, and soon his short videos were being used to complement face-to-face instruction. The advantage of video tutorials is that learners can watch them as many times as they like until they have mastered a topic.

Since its inception over a decade ago, Khan Academy has expanded its offerings considerably (Did we mention that it is free?). Mathematics is still its calling card and the lessons range from preschool to precalculus, including Advanced Placement courses. In addition to mathematics, other subjects are represented. Science subjects include biology, chemistry, physics, engineering, and astronomy. But as they say on late night TV commercials, "Wait! There's more!" They offer lessons in history, computer coding, reading, as well as life skills like personal finance and college admissions. In addition to English, Khan Academy features lessons in up to 24 different languages. We could go on and on, but instead we hope you will explore them with your child.

⟫⟫ Why is it important in distance learning?

Both time on task and relevance come to mind when we think about Khan Academy. Your child needs to have "minds-on" tasks to complete. And these tasks should be interesting and supplemental to the instruction that they receive from the teacher. Your child also needs to spend significant numbers of minutes engaged in learning. The amount of time your child has directly with the teacher will vary depending on the model used by the school system. And you can use this resource to ensure that learning continues beyond those times.

✳ Take action

Khan Academy provides free lessons. These experiences can provide your child with enrichment to accelerate learning or to close knowledge gaps that are holding them back. Here are a few ways to use Khan Academy resources, and links to these resources can be found on the companion website at resources.corwin.com/DLparents:

➡ **Daily schedules.** Suggested daily schedules for children from preschool to twelfth grade include suggested times for getting up, schoolwork, movement and exercise breaks, downtime, and bedtime.

➡ **Khan Academy YouTube channel for your youngest children.** Toddlers from age 2 and up can participate in a daily circle activity and use free downloadable activity sheets.

➡ **Resources for parents.** Khan Academy offers a library of recorded webinars on topics such as motivating children and balancing multiple children and their schedules.

➡ **SAT and PSAT practice.** Middle and high school students can take a diagnostic test and receive a customized set of lessons specific to their areas of need.

⚷ Key Messages

Learning from home can prove to be a bonus for your child when it comes to accelerating their learning or circling back to review a concept or skill they aren't yet confident in. Remember:

➡ Check out Khan Academy resources to see what catches your eye.

➡ Explore Khan Academy with your child to find out about learning they are interested in exploring.

➡ If they aren't interested at the moment, revisit it again in a few weeks to see if they have changed their minds.

➡ If you are concerned that your child is in need of more practice in a subject, consult with the teacher about this and other intervention options.

THE VALUE OF ARTS AND MUSIC

What is it?

Education is more than just subjects such as reading, mathematics, history, and science. Young people's lives are enriched and informed by the visual and performing arts. They fuel creativity, provide outlets for expression, and contextualize the human experience. Bring the arts into your home to give your child another way to learn.

Why is it important?

The arts foster curiosity in young people that in turn fuels their intellectual growth. In particular, the arts create a platform for them to expand their literacy. Oral language is the most obvious area in which this growth might emerge, as children engage with an image or sculpture and begin to ask questions and make observations. There's lots of opportunity to develop vocabulary skills here, whether through asking a very young child about colors and shapes or through asking older children about the ideas an artist may have had when creating a work of art. Drama is another one of the arts, and plays can provide children with the means to engage in repeated reading to build their fluency, all the while helping them to learn something about the world. Music can serve as a vehicle for helping children practice the very same rhythm and sounds that young readers need to develop for their phonemic awareness skills. Finally, the movement art of dance provides children with practice in both fine- and gross-motor skills and in cross-lateral coordination, which is the ability to synchronize movement on both sides of the body. All of these skills gained through creative movement and dance are also linked to skills for reading, handwriting, and reasoning.

⟫⟫⟫ Why is it important in distance learning?

Many of the outlets we've become accustomed to, such as public performances, museums, and such, are closed or significantly restricted due to community spread of the coronavirus. In addition, the amount of time that a teacher or school system devotes to the arts may be limited due to other instructional priorities. The arts are important for individuals and society, and this is a place that you can really supplement the experiences your children have. Here are a few quotes to consider:

"I am my own muse, the subject I know best." –Frida Kahlo

"All art is self-portraiture." –Kehinde Wiley

"There are two distinct languages. There is the verbal, which separates people . . . and there is the visual that is understood by everybody." –Yaacov Agam

"A simple line painted with the brush can lead to freedom and happiness." –Joan Miró

"Great art picks up where nature ends." –Marc Chagall

"A picture is worth a thousand words." –Unknown

✳ Take action

Art and music build knowledge and foster creativity. However, in a distance learning environment these subjects might be shortchanged. There are still lots of ways to view and experience art in your home and online.

➡ **Tour museums virtually.** Over 2,500 museums worldwide offer virtual tours of their holdings and many of these are free. If you have a favorite local museum, check out their website to see if they offer virtual tours. Other prominent museums that offer free virtual tours include the British Museum in London; the National Museum of Modern and Contemporary Art in Seoul, South Korea; and the National Museum of Anthropology in Mexico City.

➡ **Take advantage of interactive virtual music and art experiences.** Let your child explore percussion in hip-hop and make her own beats at Virtual Drumming. The link to this resource can be found on the companion website at resources.corwin.com/DLparents. The New York Philharmonic and San Francisco Symphony have kid zone games and activities for young listeners. The Columbus Museum of Art is celebrating textual artist Aminah Brenda Lynn Robinson's 70th birthday with digital art building materials for your child to create his own work of art. Links to these resources can be found on the companion website at resources.corwin.com/DLparents.

➡ **Make simple art supplies available.** You don't need elaborate art supplies or expensive kits to bring art expression into your home. Gather up supplies that are already in your house (e.g., crayons, glue, paper, stickers) and put them together in a plastic tub or other container. You may find that a collection of supplies is all that is needed to get your child going. Parent Sylvia Porras, a reviewer for this book, reminded us of her children's re-creations of favorite books as well as new ones they made together, using pictures cut from magazines and mailed advertisements as illustrations.

➡ **Find out about your child's musical tastes and share your own.** A recent report found that 85 percent of young people between the ages of 7 and 17 said that music makes them happy, and they rated this pastime equal to gaming and ahead of sport, drama, dancing, and arts and crafts. Your tween or teen may be listening to contemporary music that you don't really understand, but put your own tastes aside and let them educate you on what they like and why. You can also share music you were listening to when you were their age and why it held meaning for you. You might both gain a new appreciation for a broader range of music.

 Key Messages

Art and music build knowledge and foster creativity. However, in a distance learning environment these subjects might be shortchanged. Remember:

➡ Bring the arts into your home using free and low-cost items.

➡ Bring the arts home virtually. There are so many museums and other art institutions that have made their collections accessible via the internet.

➡ Gather supplies around the house and put them together to foster impromptu creative expression.

➡ Talk with your child about music so you can learn something about one another.

THE VALUE OF GUIDING, NOT TELLING

What is it?

In the course of assisting your child with a school assignment, you might find her stumped. You could give her the answer, but somehow that doesn't sit quite right with you. But what should you do? Use a guided approach to instruction to get her to do the thinking.

Why is it important?

Most of us have witnessed our children laboring over a school assignment. They're stuck, and we're not sure how to get them unstuck. There's the temptation of telling them the answer. After all, that addresses the immediate problem of completing the task. But providing the answer doesn't help them in terms of learning. In fact, over time it can contribute to an intellectual learned helplessness, in which they doubt their own ability and instead believe that help from someone else is the only solution. We are also not suggesting that the only alternative is to leave them feeling defeated and frustrated. Rather, a guided approach to instruction can be a bridge between what they know but may have temporarily forgotten, and what is new.

> **OVER TIME, TELLING YOUR CHILDREN THE ANSWER WHEN THEY'RE STUCK CAN CONTRIBUTE TO INTELLECTUAL LEARNED HELPLESSNESS.**

Any learner of any age requires practice with new skills and concepts. But the repetition and rehearsal of new skills is imperfect. In particular, what can happen is that in concentrating on the new they might overlook what they already know. As one nonacademic example, a budding basketball player working on a new passing technique may miss the rebound he needed to successfully execute in order to get the ball in the first place. In other words, a lot of learning is about being able to string together many ideas or techniques, not just about mastering one in isolation. That's the temporary forgetting—in an effort to address one problem he overlooked something else that could have led to success.

>>> Why is it important in distance learning?

When it comes to homework and projects students complete outside of the school day, there is always a risk that they get "help" from others and don't actually do the thinking themselves. When students are in school, their teachers guide their thinking and provide prompts as they struggle. In distance learning, there is a potential for parents to inadvertently increase the amount of telling that their children experience. Well-meaning adults in their lives might think that they are helping when in fact they are reducing the learning opportunities that come from struggle.

 Take action

When confronted with a problem that has stymied your child, move through a series of questions, prompts, and cues that can spark their thinking. This shouldn't be a long and drawn out process. However, a few minutes of guiding their thinking may be just what they need to jumpstart their learning.

> IN DISTANCE LEARNING, THERE IS THE POTENTIAL FOR PARENTS TO INADVERTENTLY INCREASE THE AMOUNT OF TELLING THAT THEIR CHILDREN EXPERIENCE.

→ **Start with noticing what they know and don't know.** When your child provides an answer that is incorrect, know that it came from somewhere. Children rarely give an incorrect answer that makes no sense whatsoever. More often than not, your child's answer reflects a partial understanding of something. There's a gap between the things they know and the things they don't know. What's in that gap? Ask some questions to find out. *Can you tell me more about that? Can you show me where you found that information? Why did you choose that answer?*

→ **Ask questions to get them to notice their own thinking.** Ask them what they do know about the problem they are trying to solve. These questions are mostly in the form of the 5 Ws: *Who? What? When? Where? Why? How?* The purpose is to check on their factual knowledge and see if they have any misconceptions. It can be helpful to make note of what they are telling you. Sometimes you'll find that simply asking them some questions is all they need to get going again.

→ **Prompt thinking by asking about background knowledge.** When your initial questions aren't sufficient, move to prompts that are a bit more specific. Prompts are reminders of overlooked sub-skills they need to complete the task. Often there are processes or procedures that they were taught previously but aren't using in the moment. A writing assignment, for example, probably has a checklist or rubric that the teacher has used before. It may be enough to say, "Let's look at the rubric to see what you might be missing." A mathematics problem may require using an overlooked procedure. "Are you using the order of operations correctly?" Again, the prompt may be enough for them to regain momentum.

→ **Use cues to shift attention.** While questions and prompts are often sufficient, there are times when they still aren't quite there yet. Use cues, which are more overt, to shift their attention to the information they need to complete the task. You might repeat a statement they made back to them with some emphasis on the error: "Do *some* insects have six legs, or do *all* insects have six legs?" You might suggest, "Can you reread that second paragraph? I think you'll find your answer there" or ask them to look back at a diagram or a glossary in their textbook.

→ **Provide an explanation of the answer.** If your questions, prompts, and cues aren't enough to bridge their understanding, you might choose to provide the answer. However, don't just say "The answer is 24." Tell them how you know that is the correct answer by explaining your thinking. This gives you the opportunity to reveal your own thinking processes. And if you don't know the answer yourself, don't be afraid to say so. Instead, ask them what they might do the next time they talk with the teacher. Children who can identify what they still need are learners who possess a great deal of insight about their own learning.

🔑 Key Messages

Use a guided approach when your child gets stuck on an assignment or task. By the way, this same approach works just as well when your child is trying to solve a problem at home (e.g., looking for her soccer cleats, completing chores, and running an errand). Remember:

➡ When you child is stuck, begin by noticing what they know and don't know. Their incorrect answer might have a lot correct inside of it.

➡ Ask 5W questions to spark their thinking.

➡ If that isn't sufficent, move to prompts that remind them of other skills or concepts they temporarily forgot to use.

➡ If they are still stuck, use cues, which are more obvious clues that shift their attention to where they might locate the answer or the information they need to complete the task.

➡ If they still don't know, explain your thinking as you provide them with the correct answer. Encourage them to think about what they still need to learn so that when they talk to their teacher they can advocate well for themselves.

> **CHILDREN WHO CAN IDENTIFY WHAT THEY STILL NEED ARE LEARNERS WHO POSSESS A GREAT DEAL OF INSIGHT ABOUT THEIR OWN LEARNING.**

THE VALUE OF WAIT TIME

What is it?

Wait time is the pause you provide your child after you ask an open-ended question, and again after they answer. The pauses allow your child some thinking time to contemplate and extend the answer. Wait time is a basic principle of teaching, but you'll find it is also useful in nonacademic conversations, too.

Why is it important?

Consider how valuable it is when someone asks you a question that requires some thinking before you respond, and then actually gives you that time. That's wait time. Typically 3 to 10 seconds in length, wait time is useful for children to gather their thoughts. Children in classrooms where the teacher is intentional about wait time have a lot fewer "I don't know" replies. These pauses foster the kind of language growth young children need, especially in developing their vocabulary. Young people who are learning in a new language also benefit because it gives them the space they need to switch between languages. Older students in classrooms that use lots of wait time produce longer and more detailed answers.

When we are talking, we are filling up children's brain bandwidth as they listen and try to understand what is being said. It's only after we stop talking that the thinking can begin. Of course, you don't need to provide wait time after every question asked, but it is worth doing so when the question is open ended, meaning that there is more than one possible answer. A close-ended question sounds like this: "What time is bedtime?" or "What is in a water molecule?" An open-ended question can be answered a number of ways: "What do you think is a good bedtime for a person your age and why do you think so?" or "What might happen if you took hydrogen out of water?" Providing a pause after asking an open-ended question gives your child time to think. Pausing after asking an open-ended question is called wait time 1. But there's also wait time 2, which is another pause *after* the reply. Children who have provided an answer and then enjoy a few more seconds of quiet will often add on to their answer. They use more words, form longer sentences, and give additional ideas. It's great for language development, but also for generating ideas.

> **PROVIDING A PAUSE AFTER ASKING AN OPEN-ENDED QUESTION GIVES YOUR CHILD TIME TO THINK.**

>>> Why is it important in distance learning?

Let's face it, we're all in a rush. There is so much to do in any given day, especially now that we are either working from home, looking for work, or leaving home as an essential worker. When your child was physically in school, teachers were taught to use wait time to encourage thinking. They will still do so in the sessions that they have with your children. And you can help by providing similar wait time experiences during the opportunities you have to engage with your child's learning.

✳ Take action

Wait time is useful in conversations that require deeper thinking. Asking comprehension questions during a bedtime story or helping your child work through an assignment requires more contemplation. Add wait time to your repertoire to encourage reflection. Some of the questions you ask of your child, whether academic or nonacademic, require some additional wait time to let them do some more thinking. Your questions might be during a story you are reading together, or as part of a school assignment they are completing. Consider using these techniques when wait time is of value, adapted from advice by educators Barbara Wasik and Annemarie Hindman:

→ **Model waiting and thinking.** When your child asks you a question that requires some thinking on your part, make mention of the fact that you are thinking. "I'm thinking about what you just asked me. I have better answers when I take a few seconds to think."

→ **Teach active listening.** Active listeners focus their attention on the speaker, look at them, and listen quietly for the person to finish. Show your child the value of this in your conversations and encourage them when they do so.

→ **Do some silent counting.** Notice the natural pauses you take in discussions with your child. You may be surprised to notice that it is as short as 1 second. Count silently to three or four to help you remember to pause when you're asking an important question.

➡️ **Encourage your child to add words and ideas.** Sometimes young people will answer in one word when you were really hoping for more. Asking them to "Say more about your idea" can encourage a bit more thinking.

🔑 Key Messages

Add wait time to your repertoire to encourage reflection and to support your child's language and thinking. Remember:

➡️ Wait time is the practice of using short pauses of 3 to 10 seconds after asking an open-ended question.

➡️ A second pause after they answer can encourage longer additional sentences and new ideas.

➡️ Model how you give yourself wait time when answering big questions.

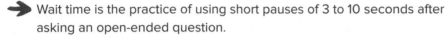

THE VALUE OF PRACTICE

What is it?

Practice is how people learn a skill or concept. In schooling, practice is key to ensuring that a learner goes from acquiring new information to really owning it. Not all practice is useful, so knowing the difference between useful practice and unproductive practice can save you and your child some frustration and tears. Without practice, the instruction that the teacher provides is not likely to stick. And practice applies to more than just academics. As we will see in the next section, we also need to practice well-being.

KNOWING THE DIFFERENCE BETWEEN USEFUL PRACTICE AND UNPRODUCTIVE PRACTICE CAN SAVE YOU AND YOUR CHILD SOME FRUSTRATION AND TEARS.

Why is it important?

Think of the ways practice has figured into your life. Do you play a musical instrument? Does everyone come to you when they need something fixed? Have you taught your kids to throw a football with a tight spiral because you do it so well? Whatever your expertise, you undoubtedly gained it due to practice. You didn't just wake up one morning suddenly knowing how to play the keyboards, fix electronics, or throw a ball accurately. You took advantage of practice opportunities to hone your skills. Practice is essential for academic skills, too. Whether it is learning to read, utilizing math skills, or understanding how chemical compounds respond, practice is how your child deepens skills.

But not all practice is created equally. Practice should be spaced and deliberate. We'll use studying as an example because it is one form of practice. Most adults have had the unfortunate experience of cramming for a test the night before the exam. You stayed up late, read through your notes until your eyes were bleary, and then collapsed into bed. The next morning you took the test and probably didn't do as well as you could have. All that cramming is called *massed* practice because you pulled one 5-hour session. But the brain doesn't work like that. You would have been better off doing five 1-hour study sessions during the week before the exam. Same amount of time invested, but much better results because your brain would have had lots of chances to make connections. Improving any skill means that there needs to be some challenge. Effective practice is deliberate, meaning that some of it is devoted to the things that are harder to do. Someone who is practicing something that is hard isn't going to be able to sustain the effort for long, but having regular short intervals is going to get better more quickly than a person who tries to do something hard once for a long time. The gym analogy works here: Short frequent intervals of a heavy exercise like lifting weights or running is going to deliver better results than working out once a month for a longer period of time.

> **PRACTICE SHOULD BE SPACED AND DELIBERATE.**

>>> Why is it important in distance learning?

It's possible that you might be puzzled by the worksheets, practice quizzes, video tutorials, mathematics exercises, or reading responses your child is doing as part of his distance learning. Recognize that this may be a part of the practice he needs to do in order to truly master a skill or concept. If you are unsure of its worth, talk with your child's teacher to find out more. Because practice work isn't occurring in a space where the teacher can observe, it is more difficult to gauge the right dosage and level of challenge. The teacher may not be aware that your child is either racing through the assigned work, or laboring for far longer than seems reasonable because he needs more instruction. There is a list of apps that are helpful for students with disabilities that allow for practice (see Figure 8).

8 APPS USEFUL FOR STUDENTS WITH DISABILITIES

Apps for learners with dyslexia

- **Sound Literacy**—Sound Literacy provides a teacher, tutor, speech therapist, or parent a tool for enhancing literacy lessons. It emphasizes phonemic awareness, phonological processing, or morphemic word building. The app uses the Orton-Gillingham method to help students recognize the spellings of English phonemes.

- **Phonics with Phonograms**—Phonics with Phonograms is a fun, effective phonics recognition game that provides a complete picture of the phonograms needed to read and spell, eliminating thousands of "exceptions!" Students **HEAR** the sound, **SEE** the phonogram, and **TOUCH** the matching card.

- **Epic**—Epic is the leading digital library for kids, where kids can explore their interests and learn with instant, unlimited access to 40,000 high-quality ebooks, audiobooks, learning videos, and quizzes for kids 12 and under.

Apps for learners with autism

- **Sight Words & Phonics Reading**—Sight Words & Phonics Reading is a wonderfully comprehensive reading program for beginning readers (ages 2–8). It is a perfect way to learn phonics, sight words, tracing, and more.

- **Choiceworks Calendar**—The Choiceworks Calendar is a powerful picture-based learning tool that helps children learn what is happening day to day throughout each month. By presenting the abstract concept of time in a structured, visual format, Choiceworks Calendar helps children organize their lives as well as understand sequence and time.

- **Verbal Me**—This easy-to-use AAC (augmentative and alternative communication) and choice board app that allows users to tap a button and the iPad, iPhone, or iPod touch speaks the button text aloud. Screen choices include yes/no, alphabet, numbers, interactive speaking clock, skip counting, opposites, world map, U.S. coins, bullying, getting dressed, using the bathroom, seasons, emotions, BINGO, body parts, life cycle of a butterfly, and custom screens with editable text and pictures.

- **Autism iHelp**—Autism iHelp is a vocabulary teaching aid developed by a speech-language pathologist and parents of a child with autism. Autism iHelp was inspired by the need for specific language intervention tools for children with Autism Spectrum Disorder focusing on their unique strengths and difficulty with expressive vocabulary.

Apps for learners with vision-related disabilities

- **Dragon Dictation**—Dragon Dictation makes it possible to transform voice to text and put your thoughts down anywhere, anytime. All you need is the app installed on Windows, Mac, iPhone, or Android phone, and your voice.

- **TapTapSee**—TapTapSee is a mobile camera application designed specifically for blind and visually impaired users, powered by the CloudSight Image Recognition API. TapTapSee utilizes your device's camera and VoiceOver functions to take a picture or video of anything and identify it out loud for you.

- **Talking Calculator**—A comprehensive featured calculator that has large colorful buttons, optional high contrast, full VoiceOver support, and unique to this calculator: the option to use speech for answers, button names, and formulas!

Apps for learners with writing difficulties

- **The Writing Machine**—The Writing Machine is designed to start introducing your child to these preliteracy concepts of print, text, reading, and writing. The Writing Machine starts this process by introducing how one picture and one word go together. From this foundation, your child will begin to understand additional preliteracy concepts including how to read text from left to right and to tell words from letters.

- **Letter School**—The number-one alphabet tracing and words spelling app for toddlers and preschoolers. Recommended and used by parents, teachers, and occupational therapists!

- **Word Magic**—Word Magic is a literacy-based app that is aimed at helping children who are taking their first steps in learning how to read and write. It is an excellent application for children to have fun with words and their spellings and learn them. A picture is shown and the children should select the missing letter for the picture. The picture for the word will be read out. Based on the child's level, you can choose the missing letter(s) at the beginning or in the middle or in the last.

(Continued)

(Continued)

> **Apps for learners who are Deaf or hard of hearing**
>
> - **Sorenson BuzzCards**—BuzzCards is an app designed to help the Deaf communicate easily with people who don't sign. The app works like a deck of flash cards. You can create some cards ahead of time that you might need to use more often, such as "Where is the restroom?" or "Where is the nearest bus stop?" Your cards are kept organized by category to make them easy to find.
>
> - **ASL Kids–Sign Language**—The ASL experts in this app are between the ages of 1 and 12, and they teach you common signs from the ASL dictionary and baby sign language. All hand signs, furthermore, are accompanied by a large image and an audio button designed to stimulate speech and hearing.
>
> - **Signed Stories**—Best-selling children's stories performed in American Sign Language with a free book, vocabulary builder, and fun learning games. There are awesome high-definition books from as little as 99¢/79pp selected to support Common Core State Standards and National Curriculum. Optional captions and subtitles can be customized and it is accessible for all children with narration, music, and sound effects.

✳ Take action

Practice is an essential part of learning, although your child may not yet have a full understanding of why it is important. Here are some ideas to develop the habits and dispositions needed to make practice worthwhile:

➡ **Help your child develop good habits for practice.** Share what you know about spaced practice and the benefits of short regular intervals over one long (and often fruitless) cram session. Whether it is homework or studying, this is a habit that pays off over a lifetime.

➡ **Speak positively about the practice work they are assigned.** We recognize that there is a difference between busy work and practice. It's busy work when your child already thoroughly knows the skill or concept and is just dashing through them to get it done. But if they are making some errors and having to struggle a bit, then it is useful practice. Learning isn't error free and should be seen as something that is a natural part of the process. Your attitude toward practice gives your child insight about how he should perceive his schoolwork.

➡ **Help him see that there is a difference between knowing something and doing something.** Children can often confuse recognition of something with actually being able to do something with the information. Being familiar with a movie doesn't mean you can make a movie. If he protests that "I read this once already!" or "She told us about this yesterday!" you might respond by digging a bit deeper about what he knows and how he is applying it.

🔑 Key Messages

Spaced and deliberate practice moves learners forward on the path to mastery. Remember:

➡️ Spaced practice of regular shorter intervals is far more effective than massed practice. Don't tell your child to do all of the practice work at the same time.

➡️ Some of the practice should be deliberate, which means focusing on the more challenging parts of a set of skills or concepts.

➡️ Your beliefs about practice set the stage for your child to understand the value of practice.

➡️ Check in with your child's teacher if the practice work assigned is consistently too easy to too difficult.

3 THE PRINCIPLES OF WELL-BEING

We are social beings. We are connected. The African proverb *It takes a village to raise a child* is true. But even in the best of times, the village can be complicated. We can get angry and frustrated with each other. We can feel alienated from or not supported by others in our community. Before COVID-19 hit, our villages felt like they were coming apart. Political polarization, more significant disparities of income, increased antisocial behavior online all made many people feel unsettled at best. Young people were experiencing unprecedented rates of anxiety, depression, and loneliness and have grown up among economic, cultural, and social turmoil along with a revolution in technology. In the United States, school shootings and active shooter drills have become normalized in a young person's experience with school.

And still, young people are remarkably resilient. And we are too.

We are going to figure this out. We will rebuild our villages by strengthening our connection and commitment to each other. We must cherish and maintain our relationships with each other to keep our children safe and healthy. But how? By grounding our decisions and actions in principles, increasing our ability to manage our emotions, and sharpening our own social skills. We are, and will continue to grow at being, the teachers and role models our children need us to be.

In this section:

- [ ] SOCIAL EMOTIONAL LEARNING IS NOT JUST SOFT SKILLS
- [ ] HAPPINESS
- [ ] THE POWER OF DIGNITY
- [ ] SEPARATING DIGNITY FROM RESPECT
- [ ] PUTTING PRINCIPLES INTO ACTION
- [ ] UNDERSTANDING EMOTIONAL REGULATION
- [ ] EMOTIONAL GRANULARITY

- [ ] ANXIETY
- [ ] SELF-COMPASSION
- [ ] MANAGING CONFLICTS
- [ ] FRIENDSHIPS IN COVID-19
- [ ] TEASING: IT'S COMPLICATED
- [ ] BULLYING
- [ ] COMMUNICATION WITH OTHER PARENTS
- [ ] POD TEACHING: LEARNING PODS

SOCIAL EMOTIONAL LEARNING IS NOT JUST SOFT SKILLS

What is it?

When you opened *The Distance Learning Playbook for Parents*, you read about the ideas that set the foundations for this book. In this section, we will build from this foundation to deepen your knowledge of social and emotional learning and emotional regulation for your own benefit and support the young person in your care to increase their emotional intelligence and social skills. Now, they have never been more important and simultaneously more challenging to maintain.

Schools provide instruction in various content areas and disciplines, but the real magic is how they socialize children. Ideally, they provide a safe place to practice social skills, receive coaching on those skills, and help children develop a sense of responsibility to and for others. As noted in the opening letter, employers want to hire people who can work together in productive ways and require that they have the underlying social skills to make that happen.

Many schools have social and emotional learning programs integrated into their curricula to teach students *the process through which children and adults understand and manage emotions, set and achieve positive goals, feel and show empathy for others, establish and maintain positive relationships, and make responsible decisions.* These skills, combined with a young person's ability to understand and regulate their emotions, have always been critical to navigating school, but will be even more essential in the current educational environment.

Why is it important?

Having a sense of belonging is key to a young person's physical, psychological, and emotional well-being. Student orientations, spirit weeks, community service, school assemblies, affinity groups, school colors, and mascots are just a few examples of what schools have done to create this feeling of belonging.

>>> Why is it important in distance learning?

This year, schools will do their best to fill the void created in distance learning, but they will need your help. Moreover, young people have an opportunity to contribute to this effort in a way they never have before. From their online classes to extracurricular activities, student government, political advocacy, and countless other opportunities, how students participate will directly impact their sense of belonging and in the best of cases build a sense of community alongside their school peers.

✳ Take action

➡ Encourage your child to join a new extracurricular activity—one that maybe they never had time to do before or is completely new to them.

➡ Ask your child to inventory the extracurricular activities they enjoyed the most in the past and encourage them to continue participating in the one in which they felt most connected to other people.

➡ With your child, choose a way for your family to support the school, especially the staff and faculty. Even the smallest gesture helps the school village to be stronger and the people within it to feel cared for.

HAPPINESS

What is it?

Before the pandemic, most parents, when asked what they want for their children, said, "I want my child to be happy." But what does happiness really mean? It can't mean free from painful experiences or conflict with others because those things constantly happen. It can't be free from failure because that happens as well, and it often presents important lessons. Not only can happiness include struggle and uncertainty but can also provide emotional resilience to be content even through hardship. Here's some good news. What makes humans happy tends to come down to the same things no matter their race, age, political viewpoint, ethnicity, religion, or class. It's one of those things that connects us to each other. So, let's define it in a different way. Consider the following five conditions as essential ingredients of happiness.

➡ A sense of purpose and meaning beyond oneself
➡ Hope of success
➡ Meaningful social connection
➡ Fulfilling work (especially if you are working with others on a common goal)
➡ A place to process and find peace

By the way, one of the reasons why young people love playing video games so much during COVID-19 is because the games provide these conditions. They are working hard, usually with a group of people, to hopefully succeed (advance to the next level) toward a common goal like unlocking new powers. Then, after the game, you can talk to your friends about it. That's happiness.

Why is it important?

When we focus on these conditions, it's also easier to see why the process of developing social and emotional skills is so connected to happiness, even when it feels hard. This definition of happiness grounds us and reminds us of what we need to be OK, to have the capacity to meet the daunting situation we are facing, and how important the lessons we are maybe being forced to learn now will positively come with us in the future.

 **Take action**

➜ Ask your child to go through the conditions of happiness and identify something in their life that fulfills each condition.

➜ Go through the same process for yourself.

➜ If you feel comfortable, show each other your responses.

THE POWER OF DIGNITY

What is it?

Dignity is the belief that we all have inherent worth. When it is the foundation of our relationships, it is transformative because we feel recognized, acknowledged, included and safe, and seek to affirm those feelings in others. Dignity is the inherent worth and value of every human; everyone has it and everyone has the same amount. Why does this matter? The second we decide that someone's dignity is negotiable, we have opened up psychological distance between people, the idea that there is an us and them. When we feel psychological distance from others it changes how we see them, what we think we owe them, and how we think we get to treat them.

Schools are among the most socializing places in our society and ought to be a place where every child's dignity is upheld. Schools, like society, can be places where diverse views are heard and experienced. Knowing how to deal with such diversity and being able to hold and understand counter views is a key for advancing a civil society. An aim that we imagine parents share with educators is empowering children to overcome any oppressive conditions that can strip human dignity and teach them to see dialogue as the starting point of valuing one's and others' viewpoints. Many teachers work very hard to model these values in schools, and when parents work alongside educators to impart these values, young people feel safer because they can see their villages address conflict productively and see the benefit of coming together to solve problems.

Why is it important?

DIGNITY CANNOT BE EARNED OR LOST: IT IS A NON-NEGOTIABLE RIGHT.

Dignity cannot be earned or lost: it is a non-negotiable right. It may seem apparent and straightforward that everyone has essential value. However, the practice of using dignity to guide our interactions with each other is actually a radical shift—especially in parenting and educating young people. While we are all born with dignity, we are not born knowing how to act in ways that honor everyone's dignity, including our own. These skills must be learned and practiced. Dignity also provides invaluable context for young people and answers their inevitable question, "Why is learning emotional intelligence and how to manage relationships important?"—because it gives us a common language and concrete tactics to create and maintain a school climate where all can engage and feel welcome.

10 ELEMENTS OF DIGNITY

by Donna Hicks

ACCEPTANCE OF IDENTITY

Approach people as neither inferior nor superior to you; give others the freedom to express their authentic selves without fear of being negatively judged; interact without prejudice or bias, accept how race, religion, gender, class, sexual orientation, age, disability, etc. are at the core of their identities. Assume they have integrity.

RECOGNITION

Validate others for their talents, hard work, thoughtfulness, and help; be generous with praise; give credit to others for their contributions, ideas, and experience.

ACKNOWLEDGMENT

Give people your full attention by listening, hearing, validating, and responding to their concerns and what they have been through.

INCLUSION

Make others feel that they belong at all levels of relationship (family, community, organization, nation).

SAFETY

Put people at ease at two levels: physically, where they feel free of bodily harm; and psychologically, where they feel free of concern about being shamed or humiliated, and that they feel free to speak without fear of retribution.

FAIRNESS

Treat people justly, with equality, and in an evenhanded way, according to agreed-upon laws and rules.

INDEPENDENCE

Empower people to act on their own behalf so that they feel in control of their lives and experience a sense of hope and possibility.

UNDERSTANDING

Believe that what others think matters; give them the chance to explain their perspectives, express their points of view; actively listen in order to understand them.

BENEFIT OF THE DOUBT

Treat people as trustworthy; start with the premise that others have good motives and are acting with integrity.

ACCOUNTABILITY

Take responsibility for your actions; if you have violated the dignity of another, apologize; make a commitment to change hurtful behaviors.

SEPARATING DIGNITY FROM RESPECT

What is it?

Respect is one of the most common words we use to communicate our expectations to young people. It is also one of the most misused. The definition of respect is a feeling of deep admiration for someone based on their abilities, qualities, and achievements. When respect and dignity are used interchangeably, we conflate the meaning and lose the power of each. Even more complicated is that young people often have negative associations with respect, because in our culture, respect is often about recognizing power: who has it and who doesn't. Young people can perceive respect as demanding their unconditional obedience and being forced to show respect to someone who is taking away the dignity of someone else. Without taking away the importance of respecting one's elders, when this happens in school, as in a family, a young person disengages. As long as we tell young people to respect others who are abusing power, they will be conditioned to be silent: from the playground, to our classrooms, locker rooms, workplaces, our faith communities, and the halls of government.

RESPECT IS A FEELING OF DEEP ADMIRATION FOR SOMEONE BASED ON THEIR ABILITIES, QUALITIES, AND ACHIEVEMENTS.

>>> Why is it important in distance learning?

While distant learning, we want students to feel as comfortable as they can to raise questions, share concerns, and advocate for themselves. If dignity isn't present and a part of their language, it is harder for them to do these things when there are inevitable negative interactions with the people at school.

Imagine a ten-year-old child asking a teacher for help because another child is being mean to them. Imagine a sixteen-year-old who has a teacher rudely call them out for being out of dress code on a Zoom study group because they don't think about the reasons this may be happening—like the child is depressed or the parent has lost their job and can't buy new clothes. When young people go to an adult for help, the most common advice they receive is usually one of two extremes. In the first example, the child might hear "Don't let it bother you/be the better person/tell them to stop." while the other extreme is some variation of "Fight back/don't ever start a fight but always finish it." With a teacher, "You don't have to like it, but you have to respect your teacher" or the opposite when the parent of the out-of-dress-code student will write a threatening email to that teacher and the principal. Although often well-meaning, these responses aren't usually that helpful. Blanket statements don't give an action plan that effectively addresses the problem, and in the case of parental intervention, young people can often feel like they are making the problem worse and will be reluctant to tell their parent other problems they experience.

Now imagine you as the parent that uses dignity to frame your response by saying something like, "I'm sorry that happened and thank you for telling me. Let's work together so you can have some control in the situation and do it in a way that upholds your dignity." This response validates the young person's experience and gives them a path forward to stand up for themselves. It gives them a process where they will develop self-respect because they handled the situation with courage and integrity.

✳ Take action

Think for a moment: What adult in your young adult life did you respect when you were growing up? How did they make you feel?

Holding that person's image in your mind, ask yourself

➡ When you think of them now, what feelings come up?
➡ Why did you respect them?
➡ What stories come to mind?

If you answered, "because of how they made you or others feel," you probably respected that person because they treated you with dignity. Even if they were "hard" on you, they made you feel that you mattered—that you were just as significant, valued, and worthwhile as everyone else—even if you didn't feel that way about yourself.

It is also fascinating to consider the teachers that had the most profound impact on you when you were at school. When you reflect on the reasons, it usually comes down to two—either that teacher cared enough to encourage your passion or that teacher saw something in you that you did not see in yourself. These qualities of sharing passion and upscaling expectations are attributes we trust parents also exhibit with their children, and well worth recalling when times get tough during out-of-class learning. It is a simple act of dignity to see more in others than they may see in themselves, and to share your passions for learning and problem-solving.

🔑 Key Messages

➡ It is imperative to a young person's physical, psychological, and emotional well-being to have a sense of belonging in their community.

➡ Respect is a feeling of admiration for someone based on their abilities, qualities, and achievements. Respect can be earned and lost.

➡ Dignity is recognizing the inherent worth of each of us. Dignity is a given.

➡ Using dignity allows us to separate someone's actions and behaviors from their essential worth. You don't have to respect what they did, but you do have to treat them with dignity.

➡ When we ground our work, relationships, and community in the principle of dignity, we can get through tough times.

➡ Make it a practice to see more in others than they may see in themselves and to share your passions for learning and problem-solving.

AS LONG AS WE TELL YOUNG PEOPLE TO RESPECT OTHERS WHO ARE ABUSING POWER, THEY WILL BE CONDITIONED TO BE SILENT.

PUTTING PRINCIPLES INTO ACTION

What is it?

Using dignity as a foundation, let's get more concrete with the skills to build the core competencies we all need to strengthen our connection with others: how to listen, ways to value everyone's contribution, strategies to maintain curiosity when we are uncomfortable, and ways to accept help.

>>> Why is it important in distance learning?

Principle: Listening is being prepared to be changed by what you hear. This doesn't mean you always have to agree, but like anyone, if the young person perceives that your judgments or assumptions stop the ability to exchange ideas, they will shut down. Shutting down can look different. From the obvious "I'm not telling you anything about my life!" to "I'm fine. Don't worry about it" as a way to tell you they don't want to talk, to merely saying what you, the adult, wants to hear. The ability to listen demonstrates you understand (again not necessarily agree with) what they said. This is a gift, and it makes it more likely that the other person may come to listen and understand you also. Right now, young people may be hesitant to share their problems with you because they don't want you to worry about them or add stress to your life. If they want to talk, it's really time to listen.

EMOTIONAL DYSREGULATION, APATHY, ANTAGONISM, ANXIETY, AND REGRESSING ARE ALL NORMAL BEHAVIOR RESPONSES TO STRESS FOR AGES SEVEN TO SEVENTEEN.

Despite their outward appearance, managing the transition to school online, giving up their expected routine for the fall, and navigating our current landscape of constant change is a lot for young people to manage. It's a lot for you, too, as the adult in their life. Lead with the idea that creating space for them to be heard, without adult commentary, is essential to establishing a healthy distance learning environment and to support your relationship with them. Emotional dysregulation, apathy, antagonism, anxiety, and regressing are all normal behavior responses to stress for ages 7 to 17. Starting conversations with the simple question, "Are you looking for advice or are you looking for me to listen?" will go a very long way to support your young person and create positive experiences with distance learning.

Principle: No one knows everything, but together we know a lot. Right now, we are all on a tremendous learning curve and we all have valuable lessons to teach each other. It is truly a village moment where we can see the importance of learning and sharing with each other. In education and raising young people, we need to integrate this principle with acknowledging that young people know the most about what it is like to receive distance learning. Yes, adults' wisdom and experiences matter, but we must appreciate and listen to young people's experiences so that when we do share our wisdom and insights, it is reflective of young people's culture—which, you have to admit, is radically different from the way we grew up, even before COVID-19.

Principle: Activating curiosity, especially when we're uncomfortable, is the key to learning. Being uncomfortable is normal when you are learning something quickly.

Discomfort is the new norm as we are working, parenting, and being in community during COVID-19. You may have had the experience of being bewildered or frustrated with the young person in your life. From acting out to withdrawing or just doing something that makes no sense to you, remember that there is always a reason for their actions. You just have to figure out what that reason is by asking curious questions. A curious question communicates that the person asking the question wants to gain greater insight into the other's feelings and experiences. We know it can be challenging at the time, but if you can remember to get curious, you are enabling the dynamic between you and a young person to change toward greater understanding, honesty, and trust.

LANDMINE!

When an adult says, "Why are you being so difficult?" or "What's wrong with you?" neither comes across as a curious question. Instead, it comes across as an accusation. If you activate curiosity and say something like, "I don't know what's going on but there has to be a good reason why you're acting like this. When you're ready, I'd like to know what it is," you have a better chance that the young person will calm down and believe they can explain what's going on.

Principle: Asking for help is a skill, not a weakness. Many of us were raised to believe that admitting we need help, feeling overwhelmed, or not knowing the answer is something to hide and even be ashamed of. If there was ever a time to realize we all need help from each other, this is it. It will benefit the young person in your care throughout their life to develop the skills to know when they need help, identify the person who can help them, and then seek out that help. That ability can be truly lifesaving.

✳ Take action

An exercise you and your child both can do is sit down and write the three characteristics you need in a person you would go to for advice. An example might be, opinionated but not judgmental, calm, and reliable. After you both come up with your lists, write down at least two people who fit the criteria you each came up with. Then you can show each other what you wrote and create a plan to reach out to those people.

A CURIOUS QUESTION COMMUNICATES THAT THE PERSON ASKING THE QUESTION WANTS TO GAIN GREATER INSIGHT INTO THE OTHER'S FEELINGS AND EXPERIENCES.

⚷ Key Messages

➡ Listening is being prepared to be changed by what you hear.

➡ Activating curiosity, especially when we're uncomfortable, is the key to learning.

➡ No one knows everything, but together we know a lot.

➡ Asking for help is a skill, not a weakness.

UNDERSTANDING EMOTIONAL REGULATION

There are a few core concepts about emotional intelligence all people should know.

1. Emotions feel like they are happening to you but are actually created by you based on your context and how you have been socialized.

2. Feelings are not facts and your brain is capable of profound change, even when you are in distress. This means that while emotions are "real" and no one has the right to question how we feel, emotions are not permanent.

3. Humans aren't always that great at guessing how others feel, despite what we may think or how well we know someone.

STOPPING TO THINK CRITICALLY ABOUT WHAT EXACTLY YOU ARE FEELING GIVES YOU MORE CONTROL, SELF-AWARENESS, AND PERSONAL AGENCY.

When you assume you have correctly interpreted how someone feels or why someone is emotionally dysregulated, remind yourself you may be incorrect and coming from your own perspective. The more we understand how emotions serve us and how we can process them, the better able we will be to manage ourselves and extend empathy to others. We all have to learn and practice. To get us started, we are focusing on three emotional regulation topics to build our knowledge and skills: emotional granularity, anxiety, and self-compassion.

EMOTIONAL GRANULARITY

What is it?

Emotional granularity is the ability to have a wide range of precise, specific words to describe how you're feeling. For example, take the word *angry*. There are many more specific words that can describe anger, such as *infuriated*, *upset*, *furious*, *mad*, *annoyed*. All these feelings have differing sets of experiences, elicitors, and require different strategies to process. Having more words to describe your feelings gives you many more options to understand and communicate your feelings.

Why is it important?

The better you are at describing and understanding the emotions you feel, the better you can understand your emotional state, increasing your emotional intelligence. You have to have a concept of an emotion to experience it. For example, you were not born knowing what sadness is; you were socialized to understand it because of how adults responded to you when you were a child. Stopping to think critically about what exactly you are feeling gives you more control, self-awareness, and personal agency. Getting emotionally granular also empowers you to decide how you perceive a specific experience. This will help you manage your emotions more efficiently when working with young people, and coach them to better understand their emotions as well.

>>> Why is it important in distance learning?

Everyone is experiencing this time differently and everyone feels different emotions in these moments. Young people need the capacity to describe the experience they are going through during this pandemic. At base, that is about having the skills to define how you feel so it feels accurate. Being able to describe your feelings more specifically also connects to building your vocabulary to better articulate and understand your experiences.

✳ Take action

When you or your child feels a strong emotion, try to get curious about how it feels physically and name the sensations. Having more words to accurately describe your feelings gives you more options to understand what you're feeling. How can you help a young person to develop emotional granularity? Encourage them to write down all the more specific words they are feeling. They can draw their feelings or talk them out with you or a friend. Whatever activity helps them design, build, and see their emotional landscape will give them increased understanding and with it an increased sense of control.

 Key Messages

➡ Getting clear about your emotions empowers you to define your experiences.

➡ Emotions are real, but they aren't permanent. You can change the way you feel.

➡ The more granular you can get about your emotions, the better able you will be to manage them.

> YOUNG PEOPLE NEED THE CAPACITY TO DESCRIBE THE EXPERIENCE THEY ARE GOING THROUGH DURING THIS PANDEMIC.

ANXIETY

What is it?

Anxiety, like all emotions, is a physiological response; it is your brain's attempt to respond to something that it perceives as threatening or something that makes you feel uncertain. It's easy for our minds to race as we try to make predictions about a world that doesn't feel stable. It is an understandable reaction to feeling like life is uncertain, unpredictable, and unsafe. And while it's true that we have limited power over the outside world, we can develop the skills to better manage the anxiety we experience.

Why is it important?

Anxiety is powerful; it can lead you to feel stuck, overwhelmed, trapped, and out of control. It also impacts your ability to view things with clarity because your brain is trying to protect you from something. When you feel anxious, you are faced with two options: either the anxiety will hijack your health and ability to process your feelings, or you can slow down and change the process so you have more control over the anxiety. Signs you are hijacked by anxiety are avoidant behavior, feelings of shame or powerlessness, and racing, repetitive, or catastrophic thoughts. You may also experience physical symptoms like chest tightness, quick heartbeat, and trouble focusing. Anxiety has a pattern that often looks like this:

1. There is a trigger or event that causes you anxiety.

2. Your mind reacts with repetitive or catastrophic thoughts described above.

3. Your body responds, for example, with sweaty palms and a racing heartbeat.

4. Your behavior expresses your anxiety: Your tone of voice, facial expression, or your body language all convey the anxiety you feel.

>>> Why is it essential in distance learning?

This isn't going to be surprising. Studies report that during COVID-19, we are all experiencing anxiety in ways we never have before. According to a report by the American Psychiatric Association, "More than one-third of Americans (36%) say coronavirus is having a severe impact on their mental health and most (59%) feel coronavirus is having a serious impact on their day-to-day lives" (American Psychiatric Association, 2020). Young people were already experiencing anxiety at unprecedented levels—it's been reported that students today feel more anxiety than students who were child psychiatric patients in the 1950s (Twenge, 2000). Combined with young people's possible reluctance to share their feelings of anxiety about their social and academic lives, you both need to know the signs of anxiety and how you can support each other. As the adult guide, knowing some basic facts about anxiety to share with the young people in your care helps you better manage your own anxiety and model healthy processing. Remember that we are not good at predicting what exactly others are feeling, so if you have an overwhelming sense your young person is anxious, that is a good opportunity to check in with yourself first before trying to tell someone else they are anxious.

 Take action

Decreasing anxiety for you or a young person means slowing down, analyzing your emotions, and then remembering that while they are real, they aren't permanent facts. You can ask yourself, "What feelings am I feeling? Why am I feeling these feelings?" Remind yourself that everyone can feel anxiety and it is very normal to feel shame or embarrassment when you realize you are feeling anxious. Remind yourself that feelings are not facts and that you have the power to choose how you respond. Remember that anxiety is physical and craves a physical response. Exercise, take a walk, meditate, do a breathing exercise. It can be unnerving for our children to see us really upset or anxious, but we can reassure them by talking about it in a straightforward, compassionate way. Normalizing and demystifying are the goals of teaching emotional intelligence. For younger children, we can comfort them by saying, "I'm sorry it was hard for you to see me upset. I feel better now that I [fill in the blank: took a minute, took a breath, exercised, etc.]. Why don't you pick out a book [or some calming activity] we can do together?"

For teens, you can modify with "I'm feeling overwhelmed because of [state general reason]. We're all figuring it out together. I'm going to take a few minutes to calm myself down, and we can talk about it if you want. Even though I was upset, I can still support you too if you're struggling."

If your child is experiencing anxiety so that it is interfering with normal functioning and relationships in work, school, family, friends, and things you used to enjoy, then receiving mental health support is essential self-care. If at all possible, include them in the process of choosing the therapist. They can come up with three questions that they would like to ask the therapist on the introductory conversation and then ask them to assess if they think the therapist is a good fit for them. Finding a good fit between a young person and therapist not only is good social and emotional skill-building for them, it also gives them ownership of their mental health and they will be more likely to benefit from the experience.

> **NORMALIZING AND DEMYSTIFYING ARE THE GOALS OF TEACHING EMOTIONAL INTELLIGENCE.**

Key Messages

➡ Anxiety profoundly impacts your child's health so it's important to take the feeling seriously.

➡ If you develop skills to manage anxiety, you can slow down, change the process, and feel better.

➡ Young people may not want to share their anxiety with you because they don't want to add to your worries—which is why it is so important to talk with them.

SELF-COMPASSION

What is it?

Self-compassion is choosing to turn toward your suffering with kindness and empathy. Empathy is the ability to understand and share the feelings of another. If we can't have compassion for ourselves it is harder to empathize. The truth is, it's not uncommon for us to be harder on ourselves than other people, especially when it comes to our kids. We so often blame ourselves for making a mistake with our kids or regretting a decision we made that somehow will follow them for the rest of their lives. But we can always repair our relationships, beginning with repairing the relationship we have with ourselves and modeling this for our children. We will make mistakes. Model compassion toward yourself so you can coach the young people in your life to do the same.

Why is it important?

Of course, we make mistakes with young people in our lives. Sometimes those mistakes are big ones. But ironically, one of the ways we can repair those mistakes is to exercise compassion for ourselves. Self-compassion is essential to have the skills to hold ourselves accountable for our behavior, treat ourselves and others with dignity, and do better. Emotions are like tunnels; you have to go through them to get over them. Self-compassion is proven to be one of the most effective mitigation strategies because it allows you to confront the situation and the feelings associated with it while also combating shame or other negative emotions that impact our self-worth when we make mistakes.

IF WE CAN'T HAVE COMPASSION FOR OURSELVES IT IS HARDER TO EMPATHIZE.

>>> Why is it important in distance learning?

Even though we intellectually know that we should give ourselves and young people a break as we live through this pandemic, we still can be hard on ourselves. We are all going through a tremendous amount of change and anxiety as the world we have known is turned upside down. We are constantly comparing ourselves and our children's online learning experience with others. We worry that our children are falling behind compared to other children their age instead of focusing on their academic needs. It is challenging to give ourselves or others a little grace. When it comes to young people and how they will be learning online or having to be instantly flexible about how they go to school, teaching them to be self-compassionate will make things a little easier for them. When you are self-compassionate, it becomes easier to be compassionate and patient with others as well. It also helps you react to your emotions while also depersonalizing their impact. Teaching young people positive emotional mitigation strategies allows them to have more agency, become more resilient, and increase their ability to be adaptable in the face of any adversity.

✳ Take action

Practice comforting yourself like you would a good friend. Say to yourself, "This is so hard, I'm so sorry you are going through this. What do you need right now?" Yes, it'll feel awkward at first. Try it anyway. When we are kind to ourselves amazing things happen in our body. Anxiety and fear tend to decrease, while feelings of safety and generosity tend to increase. Role modeling self-compassion, and in general, the struggle you may have doing it, shows your child that you are challenged by these issues, too, and that there is no shame in self-forgiveness. You can still hold yourself to high expectations while allowing the space to make mistakes as you grow.

⊙━⌇ Key Messages

➡ Self-compassion is choosing to turn toward your suffering with kindness and empathy.

➡ Empathy is the ability to understand and share the feelings of another.

➡ The more compassion you have for yourself, the easier it is to have compassion for others.

MANAGING CONFLICTS

What is it?

Everyone, in some capacity, has been affected by the stay at home orders and physical closure of schools. We are all spending more time with our immediate family, which is causing us to navigate and negotiate those relationships in new ways. Some of us are living with a profound sense of loss. Our children are similarly dealing with loss, change, and loneliness. All of this means we are going through some hard, challenging times and that will inevitably make it harder to regulate our emotions at times, so we will be irritated at each other. In the words of Dr. Bryan Harris, from Casa Grande Elementary School District in Arizona, "If you have no conflict in your life, one of two things are true: you're dead or you're not paying attention to the people around you."

There are lots of ways conflict comes into your life with a young person. So, when you want to talk to your child about a potentially charged topic, here are suggestions to remember in preparation:

> **WHEN YOU ARE SELF-COMPASSIONATE, IT BECOMES EASIER TO BE COMPASSIONATE AND PATIENT WITH OTHERS AS WELL.**

- ➡ Good or bad, the situation you and your child are experiencing is a moment, not a lifetime.

- ➡ You don't have to fix everything all the time. Young people usually confide in a trusted adult because they want to vent, not because they want the adult to fix the problem.

- ➡ Young people (just like all of us) don't usually "get it" overnight. All of us learn over time so it's helpful to manage your own expectations. Do not judge yourself or your child if the behavior shift takes time.

- ➡ Learning how to manage conflict is one of the most complex, critical, and ongoing social skills any of us can acquire.

LANDMINE!

Have you ever shared a difficult experience with someone, and they immediately started telling you all the things you should have done? Do you listen to them gratefully, or do you get frustrated because you don't feel listened to? It's the same thing with young people. Adults can easily fall into the trap of immediately trying to fix the problem by giving a young person "helpful" advice or telling them how they would have done it. If a young person shares a problem with you, the same thing applies. Respond by asking if they are telling you because they want to vent or if they want advice. Feel free to tell them they can vent and then ask for help, but to let you know when it's advice-giving time.

Why is it important?

How many of us are good at processing our feelings when we are in conflict with someone, and then communicating those feelings effectively with the same person we are upset with? Many of us have underlying and understandable reasons we hide our feelings of anger, anxiety, vulnerability, or frustration—or we don't know how to share them in ways that effectively address the problem we are upset about. We also have learned to define success in a confrontation by either being in complete agreement with each other afterward or dominating the other person and "winning" the argument.

>>> Why is it important in distance learning?

In "school" when young people have conflicts with others, they'll have less time, and fewer opportunities and space than they had in the past, to talk to each other face to face to resolve their problems. It will also be tempting for young people to get frustrated with a teacher or a student but not feel like it's worth saying anything about it. In the spring of 2020, we heard many students talk about experiencing these frustrations during online classes, and it was one of the primary reasons why they reported being less interested in school. Giving young people concrete strategies helps them feel more prepared and better able to advocate for themselves. If they feel they have more agency, distance learning will feel less like something to simply endure.

✳ Take action

We're going to give you three strategies: (1) for yourself when you are communicating with a young person, (2) to guide a young person to go through the process of managing a conflict with another person, and (3) for facilitating an airing of grievances in your family—but it works with other people too.

1. Preparing to have a challenging conversation

When you are ready to have a conversation about a topic that may be challenging, keep these tips in mind:

➡ Keep it short and don't repeat yourself.

➡ Keep it to three: What are the three things you want to get across in this conversation, no matter what happens?

➡ Be strategic: Are you and your child in a place and time where they can listen to you, and you can listen to them?

2. Helping a young person navigate conflict using the SEAL strategy

SEAL is a strategy to name the hard feelings we are experiencing, process those feelings, and then help us decide how and when to talk to the other person you're in conflict with. The SEAL strategy doesn't tell you what to say; it helps you think through how to say it. SEAL redefines what it means to be in a confrontation, and it can be used with anyone. You can even tell your child, "If you get mad at me, you can always use this strategy to help you tell me why you're mad."

> WE HEARD MANY STUDENTS TALK ABOUT EXPERIENCING FRUSTRATIONS DURING ONLINE CLASSES AND IT WAS ONE OF THE PRIMARY REASONS WHY THEY REPORTED BEING LESS INTERESTED IN SCHOOL.

SEAL stands for **S**TOP, **E**XPLAIN, **A**FFIRM and ADMIT, and **L**OCK.

Stop: Take a deep breath. Observe where you are. Decide what you need to do now to make the problem smaller.

Explain: Take your bad feelings and put them into words—be specific about what you don't like and what you need instead.

Affirm and admit: Affirm means that both you and the person you are angry with have the right to be treated with dignity. Admit if there is anything you did that contributed to the problem and need to include in your SEAL.

Lock:

➡ **Lock-In:** You want to keep the relationship or the connection with the other person.

➡ **Take a pause:** You want to pause the relationship. Think of it as Velcro; it can stick and unstick. So, if you separate (unstick) you can always stick back together later.

➡ **Lock out:** You feel that you aren't being treated with dignity, so you need to end the relationship.

Let's talk about the locking out part because it can seem harsh or too final. We understand that when young people are in a friendship with a lot of conflict it can feel that there is no way to stop being friends with the other person. A good question to ask is, "When is it OK to decide not to be friends? What would it look like to not be friends but still treat them with dignity?" We want young people to face these awkward moments and understand that friendships are stronger when people work through complicated feelings. We also want them to recognize the signs that they are in an unhealthy or unsafe friendship now, which also sets a good foundation for other relationships when they are older.

If employing SEAL in a sibling conflict, the option to **Lock** will look different. You can strategize within your household around what Locking could look like if someone needs space or time from the person they are in conflict with. Perhaps the siblings are allowed to go a few days without talking, or rules are established that they cannot invade the personal space of the other for a period of time, or that bedrooms or beds are private spaces. While this could present an added complication, during this new reality it is very important to help young people advocate for their boundaries, so they feel agency over their lives.

There's also a complication to SEAL, or anytime we teach young people how to express their anger to another person. It's called the pushback. It's the other person's response that may upset you, distract you, or just irritate you so much that you get off track. It's important to ask about the pushbacks because it allows the young person to talk about the reasons why they are reluctant to tell someone they are angry and helps them be more prepared when a pushback happens to them in real life.

Now you have a strategy to help you and the young person in your care. But there's a problem convincing and teaching young people to use SEAL or any conflict resolution strategy. It always feels awkward. Here are a few options to introduce SEAL:

"Let me ask you a few questions so I can understand what you're going through. How is this situation making you physically feel? Like in your stomach or your head? Put the feelings you're having to words. Or draw it. Just get it out."

"Everyone's probably going to experience a conflict where they lose their words or think of what they really wanted to say five minutes after the conversation (or argument) ends. SEAL is just a strategy to figure out how to speak what you want and what you are feeling in those situations."

"When you first learned to play a video game or other activity, were you good at them the first time you played them? How did you get better? Practice. This also means that you expect mistakes, and you will learn from those mistakes. You don't expect to be perfect the first time. Or even the first ten times. The more you practice, the better you get. It's the same thing having conversations with people when you are uncomfortable or angry with them. The more practice you do the better able you will be to say what you want and be heard by the other person."

3. Facilitating the airing of grievances

We also inevitably have conflicts within our families. The added stress, lack of freedom, and tight quarters makes for new challenges. We have heard from our students that many of them are closer to their siblings than they ever have been before, and they are also bickering a lot. As a parent, sibling fighting can be a huge stress for you and sometimes it's hard to know how serious the argument is. Again, here is where dignity can help you. If a young person is taking away the dignity of their sibling that is not acceptable; it's your responsibility to affirm the importance of dignity in your home. This means that while people can get angry with each other, they don't have to respect behavior that puts down others; behaviors that result in demeaning another's worth are not acceptable. A helpful strategy to calm family arguments is to allow each person two minutes to explain what is bothering them, why, and what they want to change. While they are speaking, the other person has to listen and not interrupt. After the first person finishes, the other person speaks and does the same thing for two minutes. Then there can be a round of curious or clarifying questions (we suggest you remind the people what those are). Lastly, each person will have up to a minute to articulate what they heard from the other person and what they can commit to do to improve the situation. This is best done when both parties are in a position to be able to listen, so you may not want to try this when you or your children are in the middle of an argument. It may be best to let them, or you, have some space prior to engaging this strategy and make sure everyone's phones are left in another room while this discussion is happening.

🔑 Key Messages

→ Conflict is inevitable and a normal, healthy aspect of managing relationships.

→ SEAL is a strategy to help you manage yourself in a conflict, so you are best set up to communicate your feelings, your boundaries, and affirm everyone's dignity.

→ We will all have countless opportunities to practice SEAL. So, don't stress on doing it perfectly. Any part that you do builds your skills and confidence.

➡️ Giving young people strategies to manage conflict means they may engage in more conflict because they feel empowered. While this can be challenging in the short term, learning to manage conflict is essential to long term success.

FRIENDSHIPS IN COVID-19

Friends can be everything to a young person. Friendships allow young people to process the experience of growing up and feel connected to others. It's fundamental to the human experience. It is central to the feeling of belonging that is so important to most of us. It is also the first experience children have navigating the complexities of healthy relationships and boundaries.

What is it?

For some parents, there has been a tendency to worry if their child doesn't have a lot of friends. But more important than having a large group of friends is having at least one person who "gets" us, who we can be ourselves around and we can depend on. But friendships, especially in school, have always been complex. Sometimes because of the natural rhythm of young people's social dynamics, but also because of the influence of adults' expectations.

> *We often adopt the personality of our friends as we hang out with them more and it can lead to a loss of self-identity as we try to meet their expectations (the hobbies they like, etc.). As a result, young people can be dynamic with their personalities and cause up and downs with the relationships with their parents as they try to define themselves. Jake, 16*

> *In elementary school, you're basically told that unless you are friends with everyone you are mean and a bully. So often people pretend to get along just to make things easier. As I got older, there were people I was friends with because they were in a class or activity with me. Sometimes I picked friends based on not having anyone else I knew. Sometimes I picked a friend because I had to be around them all the time, so it was easier for everyone if we got along than if we didn't. Sometimes I was friends with someone just because they didn't like another person, and we bonded. Friendship has levels and is as complicated for young people as it is adults. Sara, 17*

It's important to remember that friendships are often multifaceted. Young people can show different facades to different people. How they show up with you may be very different than how they show up with their friends. How they show up with one friend could be different than how they show up with other friends. How they show up to their friends online can be very different than how they show up in person. Young people maintain certain kinds of friendships in specific ways. Some friendships are maintained in group chats, in texts, some over social media, some by talking (in-person, on the phone, or video calls), others by online video games. They all matter. It is essential that your young person feels like you respect the importance of their friendships, even if they are struggling with them. Take their concerns seriously, offer feedback without demeaning their friends, and remember that to young people, digital connection feels as vital as in person, so avoid dismissing friends they have made online or prefer to only text or play video games with.

Why is it important?

Friendships teach us what it means to be in relation with each other. They give us the opportunity to learn how to stay in relationship with people we care about while also learning how to maintain personal boundaries. When young people, like many of us, have conflicts with friends, we can understandably struggle between expressing our anger and worrying that doing so will end the friendships. This is one of the reasons why changing friend groups when a young person doesn't like one or more of the people in their friendship group is way harder than just finding another group of friends, especially now when it can feel like you have to hold on to the friends you do have because you have so few opportunities to meet new people.

Coming from such a small, suburban community like I do with an even smaller school where everyone knows each other from elementary to high school, it can be hard to leave those who you've known for years at fear of being shunned within your friend group, much less your class. Charlie, 15

>>> Why is it important in distance learning?

One of your responsibilities is ensuring that your child has a friend, someone they can talk with as they go through this new reality of school and socializing. But of course, how that happens has changed. Young people are having to quickly adjust from the way they made and maintained friendships before COVID-19 to what will work for them now. In the spring, we saw friendship maintenance patterns emerge quickly. Some children and teens preferred "parallel play" by video call with one friend so they could study, watch movies, or do projects together. Others preferred hanging out with a small group after an online class to catch up. Others depended on online video games to maintain friendships. Others depended on long-distance relationships from camp and other places to share what they were going through. And often a young person did some combination of the above. All these strategies are great for maintaining connection with friends when the options to do so are so limited. You may see a major spike in time spent on their phones or other devices, which may worry some parents. While it is important to remain mindful of healthy tech use, if their phone is their only method of social connection at the moment, that is also an important factor to consider. This is an excellent opportunity to invite young people into the conversation and set rules together. If they feel heard and understood, it will likely decrease the amount of conflict around technology use.

> DURING DISTANCE LEARNING, FRIENDSHIPS WILL BE MAINTAINED ONLINE IN WAYS THAT THEY NEVER HAVE BEFORE.

All of this is to say, friendships will be maintained online in ways that they never have before. Friendships in school help young people feel connected during the day. And young people are worried about how to maintain their friendships during this time. It's similar to maintaining a long-distance relationship. The ease of just being in the same building or running into someone is gone. It takes much more work to be in relation with one another remotely and takes much more work to sustain relationships that miss the fleeting moments of socializing that makes you feel connected to others. Young people may be trapped in friendships since they have no one else to turn to or can't socialize at school so they can meet new people. For the near future, it looks like we really are going to have to do our best to make the friendships we have work, and that's why handling conflict is so much more important than it was before. As parents, we have to acknowledge the complexity of friendships right now and understand that they may look drastically different than we would like. Spending hours playing a video game online together or watching a movie on FaceTime is valuable time young people are spending to build and maintain friendships.

With my school we have 1400 kids total and we are going to be divided into 3 groups of 475 that go into school every third day, when we don't go in, we will be doing virtual learning. So, my main concern is that I won't be able to see most friends and other kids at school. Gus, 16

✳ Take action

How do we help young people know who they want to be friends with and how to maintain those friendships? Here's an activity you can do with a young person that gives them the ability to develop the friendships that make them feel good and supported. Healthy friendships make everyone's dignity feel important.

Avoid focusing on a particular person (for example, a child you may not like who they hang out with) while walking through this activity of creating the criteria for any friendship or relationship. We call this a *Friendship Bill of Rights* and it is an essential reference when a young person is thinking through a problem they have with a friend.

> ➡ Identify the three most important qualities of a good or healthy friendship.
>
> ➡ Identify the three most important qualities of a bad or unhealthy friendship.
>
> ➡ Think about the quality of your friendships: Do your friends treat you according to what you value in a good friendship? Are you treating people according to what you say you value in a good friendship?

If the young person is struggling with a friendship, they can compare their list with how they would describe the friendship. Just don't expect them to realize they are in an unhealthy friendship and break it off. That may be impossible right now. Encourage them to at least admit to themselves when the person is doing something against their friendship bill of rights. Remind them the smallest act of establishing personal boundaries to a friend like this is actually a really brave decision. Recognizing the state of their friendship gets them on the path to making better decisions about their friendships and other relationships in the future.

DON'T EXPECT THEM TO REALIZE THEY ARE IN AN UNHEALTHY FRIENDSHIP AND BREAK IT OFF. THAT MAY BE IMPOSSIBLE RIGHT NOW.

🗝 Key Messages

> ➡ Friendships make it possible to go through incredibly difficult times.
>
> ➡ Young people will have different ways of maintaining those friendships and all of those ways are important to them.
>
> ➡ We will have limits on our freedom to make new friends so it's in our best interest to make the friendships we have work.

➡️ If we aren't being treated with dignity in our friendships, then knowing how to articulate those feelings is essential to our well-being and ability to make friends who will.

➡️ Having a strategy like SEAL to have difficult conversations with friends can strengthen the friendship.

➡️ Make sure that the young person in your care feels that you know all the above.

TEASING: IT'S COMPLICATED

What is it?

In any good friendship there will definitely be a lot of teasing and each friend knows which lines they can't cross. If you start to notice this line being crossed over and over chances are, they are not a good friend. The sections below are really good for helping someone figure out this stuff. Gus, 16

I do feel that lines are sometimes blurred and that even close friends don't really recognize them simply because we're good at hiding when jokes hurt us—for the most at least. Radhika, 16

Why is it important?

TEASING CAN BE THE GLUE IN A FRIENDSHIP. IT CAN ALSO MAKE A PERSON FEEL RESENTFUL AND UNSAFE IN A FRIENDSHIP.

Teasing is and always has been complicated. It's one of those evergreen issues that adults and young people can both relate to. But now, when so many of our friendships will be maintained online, and we will have fewer opportunities to figure out misunderstandings in person, understanding the definition of teasing is critical to your child's ability to navigate the inevitable confusing moments in friendships. It's important to define teasing.

Good Teasing

The teasing feels like a good part of the friendship.

The teasing makes you feel closer to the other person.

You don't feel the teaser wants to put you down.

If you decide you don't like it, you feel like you can say something, and it will stop.

Annoying Teasing

You feel the teaser should know you don't like it, but they don't or won't admit it.

You feel weak or too sensitive to bring it up, so you don't say anything.

If you say you don't like it, the other person doesn't take you seriously.

Hurtful Teasing

You feel like the teasing is being done on purpose to make you feel bad.

If you say you don't like it the teasing gets worse.

The teasing is in public (in person or online).

The teasing feels relentless.

LANDMINE!

> It can be really helpful for parents to share their experiences with a child so if you were teased when you were a child, tell them. You can even tell them what you were teased about (but you don't have to tell them everything). However, avoid telling a young person that you know exactly what they're going through. You don't know what it is like to be teased on social media where everyone can see what you are being teased about. So, you can say, "When I was your age, I had similar experiences but you're growing up in a different time than me. It's really important that I listen to what things are like for you, so I don't make any assumptions and if I do give you advice it's based on your experience, not mine."

⟫⟫⟫ Why is it important in distance learning?

Teasing can be the glue in a friendship. It can also make a person feel resentful and unsafe in a friendship. As the adult, it is important to talk to your young person without making assumptions. We may see or hear teasing from one child to another that we find upsetting, and yet it is part of the natural rhythm of your child's relationship and something they use to build connection. Ask your child about it before offering your point of view. However, if you hear children using identifiers like race or sexual orientation as the root of their joke, step in. Helping children understand when their teasing is rooted in dehumanization is important. As we said above, it's important to try and work through problems in friendships but we don't want young people sacrificing their personal boundaries and feeling of dignity so they can keep a friendship. It's only logical that these dynamics—keeping the friendship even though you don't like how you or others are being treated in that friendship—will be a significant challenge right now.

REMEMBER AS A PARENT, THERE IS ALWAYS AN UNDERSTANDABLE REASON FOR A YOUNG PERSON'S ACTIONS; YOU JUST NEED TO KNOW WHAT IT IS.

Obviously, teasing doesn't just happen between friends. Annoying or harmful teasing can happen between peers like during an online class, an online breakout room, or class. When young people are dealing with or even anticipating negative social interactions like this, the incentive to miss that online class will probably go up. Remember as a parent, there is always an understandable reason for a young person's actions; you just need to know what it is. If your child starts missing their online classes, it could be because someone is making them feel they don't want to be there.

✳ Take action

If a child comes to you and says some variation of, "These people are teasing/messing with/bothering me," pay attention. We suggest responding with, "I'm so sorry.

HOW TEASING IS DEFINED IS ALWAYS UP TO THE PERSON RECEIVING THE TEASING. NO ONE GETS TO TELL ANOTHER PERSON THAT THEY ARE OVERLY SENSITIVE OR TOOK IT THE WRONG WAY.

Can you tell me a few specifics or describe what's happening that you don't like? I don't want to make any assumptions." That way you and your child can figure out what category the teasing is in and can strategize appropriately. But the bottom line is, no matter how small or how long it's been going on for, no one gets to dismiss their feelings or how they perceive their own experience.

Here's a suggestion for the family from a teenager:

Parents and children could make an agreement to treat each other with dignity in the future, possibly outlining sensitive topics that both sides would not want to be teased about. It relates to the golden rule in a way where the family trusts each other to be civil and to know when to stop. Jake, 16

Key Messages

➡ Teasing is an important part of friendships.

➡ To better understand the impact of the behavior on the person being teased, teasing can be divided into three categories: good, annoying, or harmful.

➡ How teasing is defined is always up to the person receiving the teasing. No one gets to tell another person that they are overly sensitive or took it the wrong way.

BULLYING

What is it?

Bullying is a form of aggression with the following three characteristics:

1. It is intentional.

2. It involves a power imbalance between an aggressor (individual or group) and a victim that is based on physical differences, social differences, or other differences that make it difficult for the victim to defend their self.

3. It is repetitive in nature and occurs over time. It can occur face to face, through written communication and online.

Why is it important?

Bullying is a matter of public health and negatively affects the physical and mental health of both targets and perpetrators. In a school, although the target most directly experiences its impact, they aren't the only ones who feel the effect. Friends and other peer bystanders feel its consequences as do parents and educators who aren't able to stop it. To say it another way, bullying weakens the foundations of our villages.

For many years, schools have addressed bullying with various anti-bullying programs. Unfortunately, we have sometimes missed the mark in our efforts to address it because we have tended to concentrate our efforts on assemblies and campaigns that don't land with the students (and often the teachers as well) because they are unrealistic or superficial. We also tend to rely on large group messaging around the importance of kindness, which does not offer young people a complex framework for understanding human behavior. Kindness campaigns, while well intentioned, can also be easily weaponized by young people because it's very easy for young, concrete thinkers to use the idea of kindness as a tool for social aggression and exclusion by categorizing one act by a child as "mean," and thus taking that as permission to dismiss the whole person or retaliate by being mean back. Anti-bullying programs do not engage in substantive pro-social critical thinking; they tend to offer black and white vocabulary that does not separate aggressive acts (which require attention, redirection, and consequences) from the worth of the individual who committed the act. As a parent and educator, it is essential to acknowledge with young people these dual realities: that bullying is an important issue, the way it's taught can lack credibility among young people, and there is often a belief among students that in spite of these campaigns, assemblies, and posters the bullies (including adults) are not held accountable. It's as if teaching these values without teaching the skills will stop the behavior. If you teach both, then they are more likely to come to you if they experience bullying.

»» Why is it important in distance learning?

According to Cyberbullying Research Center, while we are still gathering information about teens' use of social media and the possible increase of bullying during COVID-19, there are indicators that there is and will be an increase in online aggression. Sameer Hinduja, the co-director of the Center, explains:

> In the midst of major crises, where everyone is already on edge, hostility toward others tends to escalate along with self-preserving and self-defensive behaviors. Many cyberbullying targets will hesitate to get help from their parents. When it happens, they may suffer silently since there will not be any visual cues for educators to see or investigate because the student is not physically at school. In addition, with everyone now receiving instruction online, students cannot readily stop by the guidance counselor's office, chat with a teacher after class, or let their coach know about what is troubling them and affecting their ability to play sports (since youth sports also are shut down). Those opportunities for meaningful, connective conversations and check-ins largely will not happen organically.

Understanding how bullying happens in school is only possible if we recognize that the people who probably know the most about it are the students. This was the case before COVID-19 and is certainly the case now. One of the first ways you can do that is to ask a young person to define different levels of social aggression that can get lumped together under the category of bullying. It can also help them define what they may be observing or experiencing, which is also a way of getting emotionally granular. If they are experiencing bullying, they are better prepared to describe their experience to the appropriate adults "at" school. Remind young people that we are not born knowing how to act in ways that honor everyone's dignity; we have to practice. Part of that practice is identifying behavior of others that violates our worth, or the worth of others.

BULLYING WEAKENS THE FOUNDATIONS OF OUR VILLAGES.

Young people have as much responsibility to address behavior that negatively affects them, as they do behavior that negatively affects others. Show these definitions to the young person in your life and ask them their opinion and even modify what we have here. Your goal is to have a common language with the young person so they can better define their experiences and articulate them.

Rude is unintentionally excluding, isolating, or hurting someone's feelings.

Mean is intentionally excluding, isolating, or hurting someone's feelings.

Drama is a conflict between people that is entertaining to everyone else but still hurtful to the people involved.

Bullying is repeatedly abusing power against another person.

Then ask them if and how any of this has changed since distance learning began and how they think it could impact their (or other students') ability to learn.

❋ Take action

Don't wait until there is a problem! Your child will be online all the time for the foreseeable future. With your children's input, you can create online guidelines that set behavior expectations for your child around mean behavior and bullying.

Here are a few tips to get you started, with suggestions from Devorah Heitner, PhD, author of *Screenwise: Helping Kids Thrive (and Survive) in Their Digital World*.

> THERE IS OFTEN A BELIEF AMONG STUDENTS THAT IN SPITE OF THESE CAMPAIGNS, ASSEMBLIES, AND POSTERS THE BULLIES (INCLUDING ADULTS) ARE NOT HELD ACCOUNTABLE.

➡ Create clear definitions for all your family's online learning platforms about mean, rude, and bullying behavior.

➡ Based on those definitions, make clear guidelines about how people in the family should conduct themselves online.

➡ Determine specific meaningful consequences if someone in the family goes against these expectations.

➡ Create criteria or a list of things your child or children could experience online; if any of these things happen, your child agrees to tell you.

➡ If your child receives content online that upsets them, ask them to screenshot and/or make screen recordings as a record of abusive content.

➡ Write down your child's every single website, user login, and password. Take a picture to keep on your phone for safekeeping (Heitner, 2020; So, 2020).

➡ Is there a time of day that's proving hard? As in, your child is in a worse mood after a particular class? It may be because of how they're being treated in that class. If so, communicate with the teacher what you are observing (Heitner, 2020).

One of the trickiest situations for a parent is when their child tells them that someone has been mean or bullied them. Just like your child needs skills to manage their anger, you also need the same skills. Yes, it's tempting to rush in to protect them, but these moments are priceless opportunities to demonstrate emotional regulation and social skills with and to your child.

Overall you want to be behind the scenes, coaching your child as they navigate these challenging moments. While you are always there for support and guidance, show them that you have confidence in their abilities. It is also an essential opportunity to model using dignity as the foundation for all relationships.

Let's imagine that your child shares a problem with you, especially a conflict, they are having with another person. Your go-to response is some combination of

➤ "I'm so sorry."

➤ "Thank you for trusting me enough to tell me."

➤ "I'm going to help you think this through so you can come up with a plan to feel a little more control."

You don't have to say these things in this exact order. Also, remember that your child will probably start with generalities or only part of the story to see if you're going to freak out.

Here a few common things we suggest *not* saying:

➤ "They're jealous of you. They're insecure": This response is ineffective because there's nothing the child can do with this information. Even if it's true, there's no action plan. And you never want your child telling other children what you told them. It could easily motivate the other child to retaliate.

➤ "Be nice." Accommodating people who are mean to you doesn't look like you're being nice. It looks like you're vulnerable and easily manipulated.

➤ "She probably comes from a bad home. You should feel sorry for her." While it can be helpful to understand other people's backgrounds as a way to build sympathy for another person, that doesn't give them an excuse to lash out at other people.

➤ "Are you sure? Maybe you took it the wrong way." Without meaning to, you can come across as if you don't believe them or you think your child is overly sensitive or overreacting.

➤ "Use your words." How? What words? What happens if the person doesn't listen? This puts the ownership for the violation on the young person, not the perpetrator.

➤ "Just ignore it. Walk away." By the time your child comes to you for advice, they've probably been trying to ignore or walk away from the problem, but it hasn't worked. That's why they are coming to you. This also sends the message that they have to accept violations to their sense of safety, which is not a pattern we want to create in our young people.

What if your child says, "I'm going to tell you, but you have to promise not to do anything"? This is an incredibly confusing moment for parents. You want them to tell you what's wrong, and it's understandable to feel if you don't make this promise, they'll shut you out. However, you don't want to make a promise that you may have to break because you need another adult's advice or involvement. Instead, this is what we suggest you say:

"I wish I could make that promise, but I can't. But I can promise that if you tell me something where we need to talk to another adult, we can decide together who is the best person to talk to. And we will do it in a way that makes you feel safer and that we are working together to make the problem better."

If you include your young person as part of the process, they can tolerate your decisions, even if they disagree. What you don't want to do is take action without your child's knowledge. This is, after all, their conflict and they are the ones who have to deal with the fallout. One thing we know is young people don't tend to confide in adults who they think will patronize them or overreact, no matter how good their intentions may be.

LANDMINE!

> Don't say, "Why did you wait so long to tell me?" Even if you have no intention of coming across as accusatory, you probably will. This will make your child feel shame and create a pattern where self-advocacy doesn't feel safe, which will make them less likely to advocate in the future. If you really want the answer to that, say something a few hours later like, "Whenever it feels right for you, I would really like to know why you didn't want to come to me sooner."

Key Messages

➡ Bullying is a form of aggression with the following three characteristics:

1. It is intentional.

2. It involves a power imbalance between an aggressor (individual or group) and a victim.

3. It is usually repetitive in nature and occurs over time.

➡ Any advice or information we give about bullying must be given in the context of the child's experience.

COMMUNICATION WITH OTHER PARENTS

What is it?

The stronger your relationships are with other parents in your child's life, the better able you all will be able to support each other. You don't have to be best friends; you just have to work together and support each other during a difficult time.

Why is it important?

This is especially important because getting support from other parents gets you through the worst of times. They can help you laugh, give you advice, see things in perspective, be a shoulder to cry on, and be someone to whom you can admit that sometimes you don't like your children. All good things.

>>> Why is it important in distance learning?

You and your child's social world is probably smaller, so the better your relationships with the people in your world are, the less alone you and your child will feel. You also need to share and compare information you are getting from your children and the school about how their online education is going. However, there are some pitfalls to avoid. For example, don't compare yourself or other people's families to yours. No one has a perfect life. It wasn't possible before COVID-19—despite our curated social media posts to the contrary—and it's not possible now. If you find yourself comparing your parenting or your family dynamics to someone else's, this is a good opportunity to practice self-compassion. Trying to be the perfect parent has always distracted us from being the parents our children need us to be, people who can acknowledge our struggles and mistakes with messy grace.

> **DON'T COMPARE YOURSELF OR OTHER PEOPLE'S FAMILIES TO YOURS.**

✳ Take action

Remember empathy? Let's make sure we extend that to other parents (and any adult in education right now). Give you and the other parents a break. When another parent annoys you or makes you really angry, operate from the place that they aren't doing it on purpose. Refrain from participating in gossiping or putting down other parents or other young people. If you hear or see something bad, say something like "That must be really hard for that child or family. What can we do to support them?" Using dignity, the idea that everyone is equal in worth is a helpful way to reframe and depersonalize when you are feeling antagonism toward others. It allows you to still have your feelings but realize they should not take away from how we perceive others' worth.

What if you get angry or frustrated with other parents? Should you reach out to other parents and if so, how? Using SEAL to frame your strategy, here is a structure you can use to frame your conversations.

➡ Text or email them and ask them when a good time is to talk.

➡ When you're talking, thank them for taking time with you.

➡ Explain specifically why you're reaching out: what happened that is a problem and what you would like to happen instead.

➡ Acknowledge that you may not have the whole story or got it wrong and you would welcome any information they have that would help you understand the situation better.

➡ If appropriate, set up a time for checking in to see if the issue has improved.

➡ Thank them for listening.

➡ Assure them they can reach out to you anytime.

Key Messages

➜ Other parents deserve our empathy.

➜ We don't have to be best friends with other parents, but we do need to use each other as a support system.

➜ Supporting other parents means sometimes having courageous conversations with them. You can use SEAL to guide your approach.

➜ We are always modeling how to manage relationships; avoid modeling that using gossip or dismissal of others' experiences is a good way to deal with frustration.

POD TEACHING: LEARNING PODS

What is it?

Pod learning is small, in-person groups of students learning together with the help of an in-person tutor or teacher. Pods can be parent led or taught by a teacher hired by the parents. Many families are turning to learning pods as a way to create a more consistent structure of "school" when traditional schools can feel so uncertain, the family isn't confident in remote learning, or they have health concerns that make having a child go to school and increasing exposure to COVID-19 too risky.

Before we go further, we think it's important to have a village moment: if we don't take steps to address it, learning pods will exacerbate the inequities that already existed in our educational system before COVID-19. We are all balancing the responsibilities we have for our loved ones **and** our communities; from our neighborhoods, to the towns and cities we live in, to our country. We all want to do our best by our own children, but we also have to think about other children who don't have the same resources. They have always deserved the same opportunities and resources as wealthier children, and it is a profound loss that systemic, institutional discrimination against marginalized people has resulted in fewer educational resources for these children. It is to all of our benefit that we have young people who have a sense of purpose, feel connected to their larger community, and can see that this larger community values their education and believes they can meaningfully contribute to their individual and our collective futures.

If you have the means to hire a teacher and provide enrichment opportunities for the children in your learning pod, also consider financially supporting the education of other young people in learning pods where parents don't have the ability to provide the same resources. Include educational content in your children's learning pod that highlights equity work across disciplines from the fiction reading your children do to their social studies. Ask your "old" school what you can do to support ALL of the children in your area. Don't just focus on your children's right to a good education; focus on the right for all children to have a good education.

Why is it important?

If you decide to organize with a group of parents to teach your children instead of them participating in their traditional schooling, *or* if, as a group, you want to be more involved in working with your children when they are working at home with their regular teachers, we want you to start off on the right foot. You all want a common language and understanding for how your children will be taught no matter who or where they are learning. Things you thought were clear or just common sense may not be to the other people in your teaching pod. Conflict is inevitable. You will save yourself a tremendous amount of time, energy, and frustration if you create a good foundation with the other people you are going through this experience with. It is all about learning, your child's learning. Too many think it is about you telling them what to do, and then magic, they do it and learn. Not so simple. Learning is a struggle, learning is confronting what you do not know, learning is so different when you are beginning a new task than learning after you have succeeded with the new task—the words "It is just common sense." "It's easy." and "I don't understand why you can't do it." should be banished when speaking to children about their learning. You can also have the most amazing content, but it will likely fall flat if you don't create and maintain the learning environment where young people in a group want to and can learn with and from each other.

Steps for Successful Learning Pods

1. Parents meet together to articulate goals, principles, and protocols. You can use the principles in this book or use them as a jumping off point to create your own.

2. Parents, children, and any teacher(s) hired meet together. During this meeting, the following is done with the children: (Preferably there is a scribe: someone who can write on a large flipchart paper)

   - Share the principles the parents created with children and give children the opportunity to ask questions and modify.

   - Share the goals and give children the opportunity to ask questions and modify.

   - Parents and children establish "classroom" agreements. There is an activity on page 95 that you can use. Those agreements will be placed visibly in every learning space.

   - Schedules are agreed on. Review and get feedback on the schedule and determine when the final schedule will be shared with the group. We recommend a spoke-and-wheel approach where one person is responsible for the curriculum and what the agenda will be and then the other teachers meet once a week to review lesson plans and goals.

   - Attendance policy: review what it is and how you will all communicate if a child won't be participating that day.

   - Determine how will you communicate challenges and frustrations (see the conflict section here to help you).

Parents complete the Note to Self activity. After the activity is completed, we encourage people to say them aloud.

NOTE TO SELF

What is your philosophy of teaching and learning in a virtual space? Write no more than 100 words to craft a succinct message.

Available for download at **resources.corwin.com/DLparents**

The First Parent Meeting

All parents, if physically possible, should attend the parent meetings in whatever mode they can. Once there, we think that everyone needs to be aligned; we recommend you and your group discuss and agree on the following:

1. **A Classroom Management Plan**

   - Classroom management is different from discipline.

   - A classroom management plan outlines the procedures, routines, and expectations for all the students in the class. These include simple routines such as retrieving and replacing materials, as well as more conceptual ideas such as expectations about the way students interact with others and their learning environment.

   - Discipline, or behavior management, is a component of the overall classroom management plan and is devoted to how problem behavior is prevented, as well as the approach one will use in addressing problem behavior.

   - What will the classroom management plan be for your pod?

2. **Classroom Norms**

   - Classroom norms are the beliefs and values you and your children want the collective classroom community to abide by. What will be the classroom norms in your pod?

3. **Agreements Instead of Rules**

   - We use the term class *agreements* instead of class "rules" for a very important reason. Students are more likely to understand and agree if they are involved in making the agreements. Agreements also serve to convey high expectations, mutual respect, and an acknowledgment of the learning community's needs. A set of rules that are strictly compliance based ("Don't speak unless called on.") tell the students that you're the one with all the power, and they better listen or else. Agreements represent the social contract of the classroom community, rather than a narrower set of behavioral guidelines that have been written by the teacher or parents alone. You will need to work together to establish these agreements.

How to Create a Great Set of Agreements

➡ **A fewer number, rather than more, works better.** The recommendation is about three to five.

➡ **Co-construct them with students.** That's why we call them agreements. Even young students have a good sense of what is right and fair.

➡ **State them positively.** Beware of a list of agreements that all begin with the word "No" because these do not tell students what they should do, only what they should not. Behavior cannot exist in a vacuum, and in the absence of clear positive statements, students are left to speculate about what is acceptable.

➡ **Make them specific in nature.** Agreements that are specific in nature state explicitly what the expected behavior should be, which is a key to building students' ability to self-regulate.

➡ **Post the agreements.** Once developed, they should be clearly posted in your virtual or pod classroom. One way to do so is to put them on a chart that is behind your head so that students can see them. Another advantage is that you can refer directly to the agreement when redirecting a student's problem behavior. Young children may also benefit from picture symbols to represent each one.

➡ **Teach and rehearse the expectations.** This is a critical component for ensuring an efficient virtual classroom. The agreements should be taught during each distance learning session during the first week of school and revisited occasionally throughout the remainder of the year, especially after school breaks. The teacher or parent should model each rule so that students can learn what they look and sound like. For example, if one of the agreements is about written communication on discussion boards, model examples of how these are done in ways that are respectful and academically appropriate.

TAKE ACTION

ACTIVITY:
CROSS YOUR ARMS

TIME   **5 MINUTES**

PURPOSE ➡ **To connect feeling uncomfortable with the feeling of learning**

1.   Ask students to cross their arms.

2.   Ask students to uncross their arms and let their hands hang free for a moment.

3.   Ask students to cross their arms in the opposite direction.

4.   Once they figure out how to do that, ask them to drop their arms again.

DEBRIEF   ⇒ Why do you think you always cross your arms in the same way?

⇒ How did it feel to cross your arms the way you usually do?

⇒ How did it feel to cross your arms the other way? It probably feels a lot less "normal" or comfortable that way.

TAKEAWAY

You usually cross your arms in the same way, but that doesn't make it "right"—it just makes it what you're used to. There are a lot of things in our life like that—things we do without realizing it. Our class may sometimes feel like we are doing something that feels different or asks you to think about things in new ways. I will probably have the same experience. But the more practice we all do, the easier it gets!

TIME TO TEACH!

ACTIVITY: CREATING GROUP AGREEMENTS

TIME	**5 MINUTES**
PURPOSE →	**To establish agreements**
MATERIALS	**Whiteboard or flip chart paper**

We need to set up some agreements for our group.

So, let's start with me: We are trying a new way to learn to "do" your education. You already bring a lot of experience to this moment. You have had teachers that really taught you well. And you may have had other teachers that didn't work for you as well.

First, we are going to do something unusual. We are flipping the script. As a general rule, we don't like to answer negatively. But just for this one question you can answer in the negative because we are acknowledging if we have had teachers or coaches in the past who have treated us or other young people in a way that has frustrated us, made us angry, or just haven't worked for our learning style.

Once we get these experiences out, we will flip them around to decide what you do want and does work for you.

The first question is, "What would you like me to not act like, be like, or do when I am teaching you?"

Write students' responses down on the whiteboard or flipchart using positive wording.

Examples

Don't lecture all the time.

Don't call on us if we don't want to be called on.

Don't punish the class if one person did something wrong.

Don't treat us like we're 5 years old.

(Continued)

The second question is "What do you want me to act like, be like, and do when I am teaching you?"

> Examples

> *Listen.*

> *Get us out of our seats.*

> *Make it fun.*

> *Do different kinds of activities.*

> *Make what we are learning relatable.*

> *End the classes on time.*

Now let's turn to you: What agreements should you have for yourselves?

> Examples

> *Listen to each other.*

> *Take turns speaking; don't interrupt.*

> *Tell me what you think, not what you think I want to hear.*

Teacher note: If students say, "Respect each other." or "Don't be boring." ask them to give concrete examples of what that means.

Now let's think about some common challenges we may have working together. What if someone doesn't feel comfortable participating? Let's come up with some ideas about what to do if that happens. If you're ever feeling that way, you can always set up a time to talk to me, or you can write me a note to tell me how you're feeling. Don't worry about spelling. The most important reason for writing the note is for you to tell me how you're feeling.

TROUBLESHOOTING

What if your child complains about the parent/teacher? It's basically the same as when they are in school, except that in this case the teacher could be a parent, so the dynamics are trickier.

First, let's differentiate the level of the problem:

1. How the teaching parent made your child feel—this more likely requires your intervention.

2. Content that was boring, too hard—we would encourage your child to have that conversation with the person who is organizing the content.

3. What if your child complains about another child in the pod?

All of the tools in the conflict section will help you manage these challenges. Think of it as a two-level SEAL. First we encourage your child to start the process by using SEAL (see page 77 for a review of SEAL) to write or record the following on an audio app:

- What they don't like that's happening

- What they want to happen instead

- Anything they are doing that contributes to the problem (which again is not blame)

- What they want in the relationship or interaction to positively move it forward

You can frame your words using SEAL as well. Then your child or you can use what they have written to share your concerns with the teacher. What you want to avoid is having your child try to talk to the other person, lose their words, and then not have a back-up plan to communicate their feelings and experiences. Having them write it down is the backup plan if words in the moment fail them. Usually just having the paper in your hands where you have written your SEAL keeps you from needing it, because you know your words are there when you need them.

TAKEAWAY

- Learning pods can be incredible educational opportunities for young people.

- If you are fortunate to have one, seek ways to incorporate equity education and work into your learning pod.

- A well-run learning pod will have co-constructed agreements so everyone is clear on group expectations.

- Conflicts will be inevitable in learning pods. You have the tools in the conflict section to help you navigate them successfully.

Source: Adapted from Wiseman, R. (2020). *Owning up: Empowering adolescents to create cultures of dignity and confront social cruelty and injustice* (3rd ed.). Thousand Oaks, CA: Corwin.

4 THE MINDFRAMES

Now that you've made it this far, you have a good sense of the basics you need for your child to be successful in distance learning. You also understand how to get a good return on the ever-so-precious time you are investing in working with your child; you are laser focused on providing only the most critical, research-based tasks and supports for your child while they are learning at home. So now, let's turn our attention to developing your child's *mindframes*.

The mindframes for students that we discuss in this section are the mental attitudes and habits we hope to cultivate in *all* young people in *all* learning settings. We hope you will agree that these are important attributes for learners to develop irrespective of the nature of school. And, after we explore the mindframes we hope to foster in young people, we'll turn to discuss the mindframes that are critical for *you*—and for all adults who support the learning of children—to develop.

In this section:

MINDFRAMES FOR STUDENTS

☐ KNOW YOUR CURRENT LEVEL OF UNDERSTANDING.

☐ KNOW WHERE YOU ARE GOING AND HAVE THE CONFIDENCE TO TAKE ON THE CHALLENGE.

☐ SELECT TOOLS TO GUIDE YOUR LEARNING.

☐ SEEK FEEDBACK AND RECOGNIZE THAT ERRORS ARE OPPORTUNITIES TO LEARN.

☐ MONITOR YOUR PROGRESS AND ADJUST YOUR LEARNING.

☐ RECOGNIZE YOUR LEARNING AND TEACH OTHERS.

THE 10 MINDFRAMES FOR FAMILIES

☐ I AM AN EVALUATOR OF MY IMPACT ON MY CHILDREN'S LEARNING.

☐ I SEE THE POWER OF COLLABORATING WITH OTHERS IN PARENTING OUR CHILDREN.

☐ I VALUE WHAT MY CHILD BRINGS TO THE FAMILY AND WORLD.

☐ I UNDERSTAND THE CENTRALITY OF MY CHILD.

☐ I HAVE APPROPRIATELY HIGH EXPECTATIONS.

☐ I LISTEN, BUILD TRUST, AND KNOW HOW TO GRADUALLY RELEASE RESPONSIBILITY.

☐ I KNOW THE BALANCING ACT BETWEEN DEVELOPING AUTONOMY, RELATEDNESS, AND COMPETENCE.

☐ I APPRECIATE THE POWER OF FEEDBACK AND THE PLACE FOR PRAISE AS WELL AS ERRORS.

☐ I KNOW HOW TO WORK WITH THE SCHOOL.

☐ I AM A PARENT, NOT A SCHOOLTEACHER.

MINDFRAMES FOR STUDENTS

What is it?

To get a little academic, the following mindframes focus on self-regulation—or the ability to control and direct one's behavior, emotions, and thoughts—in the pursuit of long-term goals. Simply put, these are the habits we hope to foster in children and youth—and once these habits are attained, the result is that children go on to become their own teachers. They continue to learn independently—far beyond the boundaries of adult-initiated learning. They develop a skill set that enables them to create, innovate, and think critically.

We have organized the learning sciences research into six statements. In the sections that follow, we will explore each of these in greater detail. For now, the six aspects of students with strong cognitive self-regulation include the following facts:

➡ **Know their current level of understanding.** They are aware of their performance and understand that their current level is malleable.

➡ **Know where they're going and are confident to take on the challenge.** They understand that there is more to learn and know what that is. They believe that they can learn, with the right supports, and accept learning as a challenge.

➡ **Select tools to guide their learning.** They understand the ways that learning tools work and they know how to select tools that work for the task at hand.

➡ **Seek feedback and recognize that errors are opportunities to learn.** They don't wait for feedback; they seek it. And they know that errors are opportunities to learn rather than sources of embarrassment.

➡ **Monitor their progress and adjust their learning.** They recognize that learning is a journey and that monitoring and adjusting are necessary components of that learning.

➡ **Recognize their learning and teach others.** They know when they have learned something, they know how to use that knowledge, and they are willing to share their learning with others.

Why is it important?

Let's try to personalize this a bit more. Think about the last time you were learning something new—perhaps a language or how to work a piece of technology or how to cook a specific dish. Did you demonstrate any of the habits above? If so, you are way more likely to have learned it. In fact, just like children, we are very good at estimating our success. Returning to the effect size research, the evidence strongly suggests that we can predict with high accuracy how much we have learned and how well we will perform. The power is in creating these habits so that expectations raise and there are systems in place for learners to know that they can achieve their highest expectations.

Did you notice that this section focuses on mindframes? Have you heard about *mindsets*? Growth and fixed mindsets? The concept of "growth mindset" was developed by Carol Dweck from a lifetime of careful and precise research work. She claimed that growth mindsets, which are a way of thinking in a particular circumstance, have the power to inspire different goals and shape views about effort, but she has never claimed that there is a state of mind called *growth mindset*; her research focuses on growth mindset as a way of thinking *in a particular circumstance*, not as an attribute of a person.

When faced with certain tasks, some of us start thinking that we are not capable of completing the tasks. We flip into a fixed mindset. Others of us, when encountering the same task, have a far different way of thinking. We charge forward with the belief that we can accomplish the task—even though at the same time we acknowledge that it might be difficult, that we might struggle, and that we will likely make many mistakes along the way. Importantly, your child does not have either a "fixed mindset" or a "growth mindset." Rather, your child has developed many different ways of thinking about specific tasks, and you can help shape the way that they perceive different tasks in order to propel their learning forward. Here are some of the most common situations that are ripe with opportunity for tapping into your child's growth mindset:

- When your child does not know an answer
- When your child makes an error
- When your child experiences failure
- When your child is anxious

What Doesn't Help?

1. When you tell your child that you were never good at math, writing, chemistry, reading, art, or whatever they are trying to learn. It's really not helpful and can thwart your child's ability to engage in complex tasks.

2. Telling your child that they are smart or some equivalent when they complete a task rather than focusing on their processing of the information, their perseverance or persistence, their problem-solving strategies, their help-seeking, or anything else that shows that they can attribute success to their efforts rather than the belief that some of us just "get it" and others don't.

Dweck has taught us all that there are two ways to see the world:

The belief that one's intelligence or abilities can be changed.

or

Intelligence and abilities are fixed and immutable.

> IMPORTANTLY, YOUR CHILD DOES NOT HAVE EITHER A "FIXED MINDSET" OR A "GROWTH MINDSET." RATHER, YOUR CHILD HAS DEVELOPED MANY DIFFERENT WAYS OF THINKING ABOUT SPECIFIC TASKS,

The evidence is clear. It's changeable. But some children give up before they figure that out. Your interactions with your children can help them see the truth: they can learn. As you interact with your children, *note their effort* in complex tasks, *note the tools* that they use, *note the approximations* of success. Help them recognize when it's time to turn to a growth mindset, recognizing that it's not always necessary, but sometimes it's powerful. And as you do this, your child will begin to strengthen their ability to use a growth mindset, which will enable them to eventually internalize the overarching mind-frames critical for their learning.

This brings us to the type of tasks that teachers assign. We are proponents of rigor and struggle. Children should regularly be grappling with ideas, concepts, skills, and terminology. However, there is a difference between tasks that are difficult and those that are complex. Difficult tasks are just more work. They take more time. But they are not the type of tasks that require complex thinking, extensive background knowledge, or bringing different ideas together. If your child is asked to do difficult tasks and not complex tasks, it's time to talk with the teacher. That's not rigor. Rigor requires complexity. Rigor requires struggle. Please, let your child struggle. In fact, returning to the effect size research, a "Goldilocks" level of struggle is really good for learning. By that we mean that the tasks are not too hard but also not too boring. Please don't attempt to rescue your child every time you see the signs of struggle. It's part of the process of learning. But if you do see tasks that are really boring and they are not building stamina, it's time to advocate for more complexity.

> **IT DOESN'T HELP TO TELL YOUR CHILD THAT THEY ARE SMART WHEN THEY COMPLETE A TASK. INSTEAD, FOCUS ON ATTRIBUTING THEIR SUCCESS TO THEIR EFFORTS.**

✱ Take action

Empower your child to see learning as an active, two-way process that involves taking academic risks and persistence.

➡ **Manage your expectations.** When children view education as a game of compliance and getting a grade, they miss opportunities to learn. Your attitude toward learning (not just grade point average) communicates values about learning. Make sure your conversations with your child are not solely focused on grades.

➡ **Manage your child's expectations.** Young people can put an inordinate amount of pressure on themselves, especially when they struggle with a class. Don't tell them to "just try harder" but rather give them specific advice about what they might do to achieve their goals. And make it very clear to them that their value to you and to the world is not measured solely by grades.

➡ **Make sure they are active partners in learning.** Students are at the center of their learning; teachers and families play supportive roles in this journey. That is a very different message than what is often perceived by children, who may see themselves as passive agents. Help them develop their own goals for learning, make sure they are active participants in parent–teacher conferences, and give them the space they need to tackle problems on their own. You're there to guide, not to run interference for them every step of the way. The "snowplow" parent who smooths the way for a child does him no favors. Author Andrew Solomon says that "when you banish the dragons you banish the heroes." Give them the chance to be the heroes of their own stories. Appropriate levels of struggle build resiliency and confidence—two traits necessary for moving to adulthood.

Key Messages

Really, it's about building habits for students that transcend the current situation we find ourselves in. These mindframes are important irrespective of the format of schooling. These key messages are from our focus on mindframes:

➡ There are specific beliefs and habits that your children can develop, and these will serve them well in their future.

➡ Monitor your child and identify the triggers that lead to a fixed mindset about a task. If needed, talk with the teacher about how to address that.

➡ Your interactions with your children can trigger a fixed mindset, especially when you tell them what you are not good at ("I'm terrible at math.") or when you tell them they are simply smart, or not.

➡ Your interactions with your children can help them recognize when a growth mindset can help and how to think about challenges that they face.

➡ Struggle in some academic tasks is useful; avoid the temptation to remove the struggle.

STUDENT MINDFRAME 1:

Know your current level of understanding.

What is it?

Current levels of understanding or performance are like a GPS pin drop for your location. It's where you are now, not where you want or need to be. Being attuned to your current levels of performance helps to orient you to your successes and growth opportunities. They are not your destiny and should not be a source of shame. Instead, they should be used to establish goals for learning.

THE "SNOWPLOW" PARENT WHO SMOOTHS THE WAY FOR A CHILD DOES HIM NO FAVORS.

Why is it important?

It's important that your child understands their current level of understanding or performance. And it's important that they know that there is no bad place to be. One of the reasons that adults hide children's current performance levels from them is that they worry that the child will feel bad. That happens when we make them feel bad about their performance or when we do not help them move forward in their learning. It's akin to a gap in your work performance. Everyone knows but no one wants to tell you. How will you ever improve? Or will you have to wait for your annual performance review to find that there was something amiss? It hardly seems fair. But adults do that to children all the time.

Our perspective is that children and their families own the data. That means that they have the right to see the data that summarizes their performance. Of course, some tools used to collect data are not valid and others are biased. But children and their families have the right to the information. How you talk about the information is important.

Teachers should provide you with assessment information. Don't let this define how you think about your child. It's only one aspect of your child and we need to remember that learning, abilities, achievement, and performance are changeable. Unfortunately, sometimes educators hide data from parents because they worry that it will change the family's perception of the child. For example, if an educator says, "Your child currently reads about two grades below," a natural instinct might be to attribute the difficulties to the child. Internally, you might say, "My child is not a good reader. I don't really like to read, and she might have gotten that from me."

> **CURRENT LEVELS OF UNDERSTANDING OR PERFORMANCE ARE LIKE A GPS PIN DROP FOR YOUR LOCATION. IT'S WHERE YOU ARE NOW, NOT WHERE YOU WANT OR NEED TO BE.**

But remember, these numbers are just estimates and reading performance changes with intervention. And development of cognitive, behavioral, and social skills are not the same for everyone. If you need a reminder, take a look at the picture book *Leo, the Late Bloomer*. Children develop at different rates; the assessments show the averages. And they point to growth opportunities. Hiding that information from you will not provide you with the opportunity to help your child. And hiding it from your child will not allow your child to set goals and develop self-regulation. So, what should you do?

First, make sure you have accurate information. Ask for current levels of performance. And resist the urge to attribute the current levels you see to your child's abilities. Second, talk with your child about the data. Ask your child what the data mean. If you are not sure, ask the teacher to explain the data to you. Make sure that your child knows that you are not disappointed. Adopt a frame of mind that this is a worthy challenge and one that will result in better outcomes for your child. Again, you do not have to be the teacher. But you can help your child understand their current performance level and that you are supportive of their learning journey. Third, talk with your child about a nonacademic performance indicator, such as sports, music, art, paddle boarding, or anything else they care about. Were they always as good as they are now? Did they understand their current level of performance so that they could identify areas of growth? Make the connection that it's the same in academics. Learning is about changing and growing, and these examples help children recognize that it's a journey.

✳ Take action

→ **Assemble a folder your child has access to.** Do you have a folder, digitally or as hard copies, with information about your child's academic, social, emotional, physical, and behavioral growth? If not, why not? You should. After all, you are the keeper of your child's history, not the school. Create a child-friendly version that she can add items to, including schoolwork she is proud of. Young children who aren't yet reading and writing love to look at pictures of themselves when they were smaller. Share these with your child and talk about all the things he can do now but couldn't do at the time.

➔ **Be a strength-spotter.** Identify some of the areas of success represented in the data and talk about that. Do not limit your conversation to the areas needed for growth, as it could create an imbalance in understanding oneself as a learner. Make sure that you take some time to note progress from the past, areas that are strong, or areas that are of interest.

➔ **When confronted with a problem, help them assess what they already know.** These mindframes are not limited to academic work; they are useful in life. When your children have to tackle challenges and are not sure how to move forward, encourage them to take an inventory of what they already know or know how to do. This can serve as a springboard for them to figure out their next steps.

> TALK WITH YOUR CHILD ABOUT A NONACADEMIC PERFORMANCE INDICATOR, SUCH AS SPORTS, MUSIC, ART, PADDLE BOARDING, OR ANYTHING ELSE THEY CARE ABOUT. WERE THEY ALWAYS AS GOOD AS THEY ARE NOW?

🔑 Key Messages

The next mindframe sets children on the path to closing the gap between their current level of understanding or performance and where they want to, or need to, be. These are key messages for knowing their current level of understanding:

➔ Collect and organize performance data about your child. As they get older, help them take responsibility for the data.

➔ Talk with your child about their current levels of performance. Ensure that they understand that it's about the future growth opportunities.

➔ Be a strength-spotter and teach your child to recognize both strengths and areas for growth.

➔ Revisit these data as learning and growth occur so that knowing your current level of understanding becomes a habit that is natural. This will serve your child well into the future.

STUDENT MINDFRAME 2:

Know where you are going and have the confidence to take on the challenge.

What is it?

There are two parts to this mindframe that play nicely together. The first part relates to the destination, recognizing that there are many ways to get where you are going. Some take longer. Some include detours. And some routes are more direct. That should not matter. The fact that you have arrived safely is what matters. The second part of this focuses on confidence. Overly confident students actually learn less, but optimistically confident students learn more. Importantly, confidence develops with experience, which is one of the roles that you can play.

Why is it important?

Knowing where they are going, and knowing why it's important, drives attention and encourages children to allocate resources, such as time and effort, to accomplish their goals. When school is a random collection of tasks, children may become compliant, and they may even learn something from the tasks, but they do not develop the habits of mind that we're looking for. They need to know the destination, based on their current level of understanding or performance, and estimate how much effort it will take to reach the goal.

The teacher should be clear about what students need to learn each day. We talked about that in Chapter 1 when we focused on the three questions: *What am I learning today? Why am I learning it? How will I know that I learned it?* These questions help students understand why they are being asked to complete certain tasks and assignments. And they can judge the amount of effort that will be required to accomplish it. Essentially, they will engage in an internal return on investment assessment. In an age-appropriate way, they will assess if the return is worth the investment. If not, they will ignore the task, copy from someone else in an attempt to please the teacher, or submit inferior work. When they understand the value of the destination, they are more likely to engage.

What can you do to support this? Perhaps ask your child what they will be learning in school that day. Talk about the destination and why it is important. If the destination is not clear, ask the teacher the three clarity questions presented above. We're partners in this and, unfortunately, sometimes teachers forget to share the learning intentions, assuming that students will infer what they are supposed to learn.

Confidence is another matter. Confidence grows over time and your child's confidence will likely vary highly across different subject areas. For example, a child may be very confident with their mathematical prowess but not confident in their writing. Or a child may be confident in social relationships with peers and not confident in academics. And still another child may be confident in reading but not confident in reading for information.

> **PRACTICE AND CONFIDENCE ARE COUSINS. IN FACT, PRACTICING AND THEN EXPERIENCING SUCCESS IS MOTIVATING.**

One of the ways to build confidence is to practice. As we noted in Section 2, practice is important. What we didn't say then, which we will say now, is that practice and confidence are cousins. In fact, practicing and then experiencing success is motivating. As a child experiences success, they are much more likely to engage in similar, and increasingly complex, tasks.

In addition, confidence is built through feedback and risk taking. Children need to try things that are a little beyond what they believe they can do and then receive feedback about what worked and what they could try next time. In a large sense, this is what teachers do each day. You can help. Encourage your child to try things that are a little outside of their comfort zone and then provide feedback about the experience. Sometimes, we need to get out of our own way to grow. And please, teach your child to focus on themselves and not on a hypothetical and judgmental audience.

✳ Take action

➡ *Set individual and family goals.* Make goal-setting a part of the way your family works together. You might identify a purchase and set up a jar labeled "Family Fund" for depositing spare change. Share a health goal you have, such as running or lowering your blood pressure, and keep track of your progress so that your child can follow your journey. Set daily task-oriented goals with young children (e.g., feed the fish, put away the toys in the living room) and write them down so they can check them off.

➡ *Set a monthly challenge goal with your child.* We are fans of the monthly healthy living challenge goals we receive on our smartphones. Importantly, they are attuned to where we are now individually—it's not the same goal for everyone, but rather one designed for improvement. As each month draws to a close, talk with your child about a goal she has for herself for the following month. It might be an academic one like reading a certain number of books, or a nonacademic one such as eating more vegetables, planting herbs in the window flower box, or planning a family outing.

 Key Messages

Learning is a journey and there are many pathways to success. But knowing where you are going and developing confidence along the way is important. These are the key messages:

➡ Ensure your child knows the learning expectations for each lesson. Talk with them about the learning goals and why they are important.

➡ Encourage your child to set goals, even if the teachers do not do this. Ask your child each day what the goals for learning are.

➡ Ensure that your student engages in sufficient practice so that confidence is built.

➡ Be encouraging of your child's academic risk taking. Talk about focusing on yourself and not comparing yourself to others.

> WE LEARN FROM OUR MISTAKES. DO YOU BELIEVE THAT? IF SO, WHY DO WE SO OFTEN TRY TO PREVENT CHILDREN FROM MAKING MISTAKES?

STUDENT MINDFRAME 3:

Select tools to guide your learning.

What is it?

There are a wide variety of tools that students can use to guide their learning. In most cases, there is not simply one tool that will work. Teachers introduce a number of tools to their students, such as procedures, graphic organizers, ways to take notes, and decision-making processes. Over time, they then should allow them to select tools that work for them and the task at hand. Yes, sometimes teachers need students to complete a task in a specific way so that they can assess understanding. But in the long run, children need to know that there are options and that they need to take responsibility for their choices.

Why is it important?

First and foremost, this mindframe builds children's responsibility for their learning. Tools are under their control. Yes, they need to be taught a range of tools and then provided chances to use them. Here's a little secret. There is no one right way to teach something. We do not tell teachers how to teach. Instead, we ask them to determine the impact that their efforts have on students. Sure, there are wrong ways to teach, but there is no one right way. This can be frustrating for children as some of them just want to get it right and do it the same exact way that the teacher did. And when you show them a different way, they might tell you that you don't know how to do it. Resist the urge to correct them. Instead, ask them how they did it and whether or not it worked.

Of course, sometimes children will select the wrong tool. Let them. It's a learning opportunity. We learn from our mistakes. Do you believe that? If so, why do we so often try to prevent children from making mistakes? They need to select learning tools and see if they work. And if they don't, they need help figuring out why and which tool might work. In this respect, our goal is to have children know what to do when they don't know what to do.

> CHOICES ALLOW US TO EXERT A LITTLE CONTROL ON THE WORLD. AND CHILDREN ARE LOOKING FOR THAT EXACT OPPORTUNITY.

Further, choice is motivating. We all know that. When given a choice, we are more likely to engage because we have a commitment to our selection. Choices allow us to exert a little control on the world. And children are looking for that exact opportunity. Of course, this can be taken too far. Do you want to go to bed at your bedtime? Not a choice. Do you want to apologize for your actions that hurt someone's feelings? Not a choice. Do you want to read this book or that one? Choice. Do you want to use a graphic organizer or a note page? Choice.

In addition, selecting tools for learning contributes to cognitive flexibility. Cognitive flexibility is an executive function in the brain. It's the ability to switch between thinking about different concepts or ideas, or to think about the relationships between ideas, or to think about other ways to solve a problem or complete a task. People with higher levels of cognitive flexibility tend to be more entrepreneurial, creative, and innovative. In other words, it's worth the effort to foster this ability. It can be frustrating, at first, when you ask your child to solve a problem in a different way. But it can become very rewarding.

In the case of learning tool selection, children who take responsibility for their choices, especially when they consider several and then select one, are practicing the main aspects of cognitive flexibility, namely task switching and cognitive shifting. We won't take any more time to delve into the academic side of this, so suffice it to say that choice in learning tools and the conversations around the choices are powerful.

What can you do? Refrain from telling your child that there is one way to do things, especially learning tasks. If you see a shortcut, you can make an offer, but allow the child to choose. Alternatively, you can allow the child to finish and then show them different options. If possible, ask the child to solve a problem a different way. For example, if the child solves a mathematics problem with numbers and an algorithm, ask if they can solve it with an image or with objects or with words. And finally, you can support teachers in encouraging students to have choices in their learning strategies.

 Take action

→ **Promote tool selection choices.** If your child is younger, ask them to help you choose which tool would be better to accomplish a task. In the kitchen, ask about cooking tools. "I'm making salsa for a snack tonight. Which bowl would be better for me to use?" When making simple household repairs, ask about the tools you might need for the job. "I'm going to fix the broken wooden chair leg. What tools should I take with me?"

Older children can assist in making decisions about what items need to be taken for an outing, not just gathering them at your direction. Your child should also be responsible for managing his belongings for school and other events. This builds a foundation of cognitive flexibility and a habit of understanding that there is often more than one path to success.

→ **Foster study skills that rely on several cognitive tools.** There are several components to studying, but your child may know only one way. For example, lots of students think that underlining and highlighting are how you study. Those techniques are good when you're initially learning something, but they are not very effective when studying for an exam. Introduce your child to flashcards (paper or digital) for studying facts and vocabulary definitions. Annotation, which includes making notes and writing out questions about a reading, is especially effective. By the way, doing so on paper rather than a screen increases retention. There are also several affective study skills, which are those that impact emotion and perception. For example, studying in a quieter environment increases attention. If study space is at a premium, it is useful for her to play music without lyrics (the words compete for attention) through headphones. And make sure your child understands the benefits of spaced and deliberate practice in learning.

REFRAIN FROM TELLING YOUR CHILD THAT THERE IS ONE WAY TO DO THINGS, ESPECIALLY LEARNING TASKS.

Key Messages

Helping your child take ownership of their learning requires that they make informed selections. That means they have to understand the options and be given a chance to choose. These are the key messages:

→ Children need to be introduced to a variety of learning tools, not too many, but more than a few.

→ Children need to be provided an opportunity to choose learning tools and to learn from the mistakes they make from these choices.

→ Children need time to process and reflect on their choices.

STUDENT MINDFRAME 4:

Seek feedback and recognize that errors are opportunities to learn.

 **What is it?**

We discussed the power of feedback in Section 2. And we noted the ways in which feedback can be provided. This mindframe is a little different. Not all feedback is received. You know that you have been immune to some of the feedback you have received from others. There is a difference between feedback that is sent and feedback that is received. And one of the ways to increase the likelihood that feedback is received is to ensure that it is requested. Thus, we need to teach children to seek out feedback and not wait passively for it.

In addition, we would all benefit if we could accept the fact that errors are opportunities to learn. If an hour goes by in a classroom and there are no errors, the students already knew all that stuff. As we noted earlier, there is evidence that between 40 percent and 60 percent of the minutes children are in school are spent on things that they have already learned. When we get students into the Goldilocks struggle, they are more likely to make errors, and then they have an opportunity to learn from those errors.

Why is it important?

Seeking feedback is a skill. And one that can be learned. Unfortunately, it's not taught frequently in school. Instead, teachers tend to give feedback in large part because they received feedback when they were in school. We need to flip the script here. To start, ask your child, "On what would you like my feedback?" At first, they are likely to say "everything" or "this problem." Over time, ask your child for more specifics. Where in the paper do you need my feedback? Which part of the problem is causing the trouble and what have you tried?

WE NEED TO TEACH CHILDREN TO SEEK OUT FEEDBACK AND NOT WAIT PASSIVELY FOR IT.

Then, encourage your child to seek feedback from the teacher. You may have a brief conversation each week with your child asking them to identify an area in which they would like to seek feedback from their teacher. They could even keep a notebook of potential ideas and, when the time is right, ask for the feedback. The idea is to develop a help-seeking habit in which your child knows that it is perfectly acceptable to seek help from others. The reason that most children do not seek help or feedback is that they don't want to look dumb. That's because of the culture we have created where right answers are celebrated and already knowing stuff is privileged. Making mistakes or not knowing something is a source of embarrassment and shame.

It's a problem because spending time on what is already known limits the growth potential of students. There are so many children who achieve well but do not make progress during the year. In essence, at the start of the year some students have already demonstrated mastery of the learning expectations and school is holding them back. Others don't want to look dumb in comparison, so they don't ask for help. Mistake. Mistake. Mistake. Errors should be celebrated.

As a parent, watch your body language and attitude when your child makes an error or is confused. Try to notice the feelings of frustration that may arise. Stop and try to understand that this is actually the very moment you've been waiting for. It's the learning opportunity. Your investment right at that moment is much more likely to impact your child's learning. Make sure that your child knows that errors are expected, natural, and useful. Make sure that your child knows that you expect errors and that you will actively work to ensure that there are tasks and assignments that provoke errors so that they can learn. You may even start a family tradition focused on the best error of the day. Normalize error making and the learning that comes from it.

> **DEVELOP A HELP-SEEKING HABIT IN WHICH YOUR CHILD KNOWS THAT IT IS PERFECTLY ACCEPTABLE TO SEEK HELP FROM OTHERS.**

✳ Take action

➡ **Make struggle productive.** Make sure that your children have opportunities to engage with struggle in productive ways by creating tasks that have a clear success target. Task your children with solving a household problem every week that is developmentally appropriate for them to do. "The thermostat needs new batteries. Work with your brother to figure out how to take care of this." Then step back and don't guide them too much. "Where are the batteries? What kind of batteries does it need? How do you get the thermostat cover off?" Let them figure out these answers. It won't be the fastest way to get something done, but it gives them experience in seeing how lots of small errors lead to success.

Other ideas are buying stamps at the post office, putting picture books onto a new bookshelf, making a shopping list that will take care of each person's packed lunch next week, planning a family dinner consisting only of round foods, replacing the light bulb in a lamp, or cleaning the inside of the family car.

➡ **Ask your child for advice.** Seeking help and feedback are two critical dispositions for success in life. Don't unburden yourself on your child but let him know when you're facing a problem and ask him for advice. You'll send two important messages. The first is that challenges are a normal part of life. The second is that you signal how much you value him as a person.

 **Key Messages**

Normalizing errors is an important shift if students are to learn to self-regulate. And seeking feedback is a valuable skill for all of us to learn. These are the key messages:

➡ Ask your child about the feedback they would like before you jump in and correct their work.

➡ Teach your child to seek feedback from teachers. Practice small at first and build the habit over time.

➡ Change your attitude about errors and make it obvious to your children that mistakes are opportunities to learn.

STUDENT MINDFRAME 5:

Monitor your progress and adjust your learning.

What is it?

We monitor a lot of things in our lives, such as how many calories we consume or how many steps we have taken. We use that information to make adjustments to reach our goals. If you want to take 10,000 steps, but the data say you're still at 8,500, you have to decide to get out of the chair and walk more. The same is true academically. The difference is that mostly the teachers monitor progress and adjust learning experiences. Children who have high levels of self-regulation learn to do this as well. The key is to collect information that is useful and then do something with it.

MAKE SURE THAT YOUR CHILD KNOWS THAT YOU EXPECT ERRORS AND THAT YOU WILL ACTIVELY WORK TO ENSURE THAT THERE ARE TASKS AND ASSIGNMENTS THAT PROVOKE ERRORS SO THAT THEY CAN LEARN.

Why is it important?

In a word, ownership. Whether you are five, fifteen, or fifty-five, you should know how to monitor the progress you are making. You don't have to create all your own tools. After all, we use wearable devices someone else designed to track our movement. But you do have to have a system for monitoring. Hopefully, the teacher will provide your child with appropriate tools. These can come in the form of checklists, rubrics, or a host of other options. The tool itself is not important. It's using the tool that matters.

That's where you can come in. Talk with your child about their progress and ask how they are monitoring their own development. This doesn't have to be a daily thing, but a regular one. It's really helpful if the tools used to monitor progress have indicators of success along the way. We shouldn't wait to notice that we have been successful until the end. Checkpoints along the way can be motivating and re-assuring that we're on the right track. If not provided by the teacher, you can create a simple tool to help your child monitor their progress. Here's an idea (and a downloadable copy of this tool is available on the companion website):

Learning Goal	Date	Need Help	Need Practice	Independent	Can Teach It
		☐ I am just learning	☐ I am almost there	☐ I own it	☐ I am a pro
		☐ I am just learning	☐ I am almost there	☐ I own it	☐ I am a pro
		☐ I am just learning	☐ I am almost there	☐ I own it	☐ I am a pro

online resources ⟋ Available for download at **resources.corwin.com/DLparents**

In addition to monitoring the goal, children need to know that they can make adjustments to their learning plans if they are not making progress. Sometimes they need permission to adjust their learning plan. If it's not working, then make sure that they know that they can change it up.

They may also need to invest in some study skills. There are any number of ways to study from reviewing notes to focusing on key terms to annotating a text. If one tool is not working, invite your child to change it. But make sure you talk about why it's not working. And ask them if the new choice is more useful and why. It's an opportunity to reflect on learning and not simply getting things done. To spur your thinking, we have provided a sample list of learning tools that your child might use.

Study Skills

I can take notes.

I can make a plan for my project.

I can be excited to learn.

I can use a graphic organizer.

I can keep track of my own learning.

I can make sure I am in a good spot to learn.

I can summarize what I read.

I can correct my mistakes.

I can make sure I have enough time for my assignment.

I can make flashcards.

I can make changes to my work.

I can get through a challenge.

I can reread.

I can self-assess my work.

I can set goals.

I can memorize important information.

I can use self-questioning.

I can be ready to solve problems.

I can keep track of my understanding.

I can review vocabulary words to make sure I know what they mean.

I can use my comprehension strategies when I am not sure that I understood what I read.

Source: Fisher, D., Frey, N., Hattie, J., & Flories, K. (2019). *Becoming an assessment-capable visible learner, grades 3–5. Learner's notebook.* Thousand Oaks, CA: Corwin.

✳ Take action

→ **Check in on the goals you and your child set.** Remember the individual and family goals we discussed in Mindframe #2? Have some intermittent check-in points to monitor progress and make adjustments. If it is a monthly goal, establish check-ins at the end of the first week and the third week. Longer- and shorter-term goal check-ins should be adjusted accordingly. A good basic rule is that younger children benefit from shorter goals and more frequent check-ins.

→ **Don't misinterpret an adjustment as a sign of failure.** Sometimes a goal that is initially set may prove to be a mismatch and in need of being changed a bit. That's okay, and make sure your child knows that, too. Monitoring progress toward a goal invariably comes with some adjustments along the way. When your child undershoots or overshoots on a goal, they are also learning how to better calibrate between goal setting and goal completion.

→ **Keep a visual tool for your child to monitor progress.** You know those lines at public attractions that are roped off so that people snake around a pathway until they get to the entrance? In addition to providing some order and organization, those lines work on a psychological level. Every time you turn a corner, you actually get a little subconscious reward because you made interim progress toward your goal of getting to the entrance. Visual cues that allow your child to keep track of progress accomplish a similar function. A checklist on the refrigerator, a running total on the kitchen bulletin board, or a door message board on your child's bedroom door—all of these work well in providing a visual reminder of their progress.

 ## Key Messages

Monitoring is an important aspect of self-regulation. And learning to adjust actions to reach a goal is another important life skill. Your child was not born with the ability to do this. It's taught and practiced. These are the key messages:

→ Adopt, adapt, or develop tools that your child can use to monitor their progress in learning.

→ Engage in conversations about the progress your child is making, attributing success to the efforts put forth.

→ Give your child permission to make adjustments in their learning plan. And provide options for ways to accomplish the learning.

STUDENT MINDFRAME 6:

Recognize your learning and teach others.

What is it?

The final student mindframe requires that children learn to think about their thinking. In the academic world, it's known as *metacognition*. But it's easier to say thinking about thinking. As children become more reflective, they recognize that learning has occurred and that their efforts resulted in their success. They don't attribute their learning to others; they realize they are the cause of it. Of course, others helped, but they come to understand that they can continue to learn.

Why is it important?

Recognizing that you have learned something is an important skill. First, it signals that you're ready for something else. There is no longer the need to devote cognitive resources that way. Second, success breeds success, and when a child realizes that they have learned something, they are more likely to want to learn more. And third, when a child realizes that they have learned something, they are excited and want to talk with others about it. Thus, we recommend that you stop asking your child "What did you do today?" and instead ask "What did you learn today?"

TEACHING SOMETHING TO SOMEONE ELSE ALLOWS YOU TO LEARN IT TWICE.

Of course, there are levels of learning. At a lower level, the child has acquired knowledge, skills, and concepts. Eventually, the child is able to consolidate their learning and perform consistently across time. Eventually, the child's learning will generalize to different contexts, which we call transfer of learning. That means that they are applying their learning to a new situation. Practice is important to ensure that students own this level of learning. You can help with this by creating situations in which your child can apply their knowledge in different situations and at different times. For example, while learning to read, recognizing letters or sight words can be practiced throughout the home at different times of day. Engaging in collaborative conversations is not reserved for a Zoom meeting; children can practice with their friends and siblings.

Once a child has learned something, teaching it to someone else can assist in transfer or ownership of that learning. The effect size research is pretty clear about this. Peers tutoring each other is beneficial to both. As the adage suggests, teaching something to someone else allows you to learn it twice. You can set up opportunities for your child to teach others, perhaps younger siblings. There's also an opportunity for your child to teach others in the neighborhood, virtually and without the teacher present. It's even been shown that reading to a pet can boost reading skills.

Finally, we have argued that there are mindframes that children need to develop. Thus, learning should not be limited to the content in the classroom. You can be more explicit about the habits that your child needs to develop by asking them to reflect on their developing mindframes. Here's a sample tool to do so (and a downloadable copy is available on the companion website):

Self-ReportCard:_____ **Date:**_____

Topic: _____ **Grade I Give Myself:** _____

Rate yourself on the following:

Mindframes	Novice 😕	Apprentice 🙂	Practitioner ❓	Pro 😃
I know *what* I am supposed to be learning.				
I know what *success* looks like.				
I know what my *performance* is like compared to what I need to learn.				
I *know what tools* are available to help me.				
I *select tools* to help me reach my goals and own my learning.				
I *monitor* my own progress.				
I seek out and use *feedback*.				
I *achieved* the learning goals.				

Grow	Glow
🌱	☀️

I want my teacher to know . . .

✳ Take action

→ **Encourage your child to teach you something they have learned in school.** Reinforce accomplishments your child has completed by asking them to teach you something they learned. Small children who are just learning to read are delighted to read aloud to you. If your child has been studying about the Glorious Revolution of 1688, ask him why it got that name. It doesn't matter whether you already know something they have just learned. The point is to provide another opportunity to reinforce knowledge. In doing so, you instill a sense of pride and communicate how much you value him.

→ **Encourage your child to teach the family something they have learned on their own.** Television talk show host David Letterman used to have an occasional feature called "Stupid Human Tricks." If you watched these, you realized that most of them were not stupid at all but were certainly unique. Host a monthly family night where everyone gets to teach the rest of the family a "human trick." Members of the family might learn a magic trick, how to hang a spoon on their noses, how to make a balloon animal, a hair braiding technique, or a feature on the smartphone that no one else knows about.

 Key Messages

Using a tool like the one on the previous page allows you to get a glimpse inside your child's mind and it provides them an opportunity to consider learning on a larger scale. The point is that mindframes are habits that extend beyond the current learning expectations. They are useful as we grow and develop. They're even likely for you in your workplace.

Recognizing that you have learned something is motivating. It's worth the time and effort because it builds habits that are useful beyond the current year. These are the key messages:

→ Children need tools to recognize that they have learned something.

→ Talk with your child about learning, not about doing.

→ Ensure that your child has practice opportunities so that the learning transfers.

→ Create opportunities for your child to teach others things that they have learned.

THE 10 MINDFRAMES FOR FAMILIES

We have focused on the mindframes that we hope to develop in young people so that they become their own teachers, or in the language of schools, lifelong learners. Mindframes are ways of viewing the world, ways of thinking that can help frame how you see, talk with, and listen to your children. Below are 10 mindframes that can help you assist your child in their learning regardless of the structure of the school—distance, blended, or in person.

1. I am an evaluator of my impact on my children's learning.

2. I see the power of collaborating with others in parenting our children.

3. I value what my child brings to the family and world.

4. I understand the centrality of my child.

5. I have appropriately high expectations.

6. I listen, build trust, and know how to gradually release responsibility.

7. I know the balancing act between developing autonomy, relatedness, and competence.

8. I appreciate the power of feedback and the place for praise as well as errors.

9. I know how to work with the school.

10. I am a parent, not a schoolteacher.

In the sections that follow, we will briefly explore how each of these mindframes is woven into your ways of thinking.

> **WE SHOULDN'T FOCUS NARROWLY ON GRADES WHILE OVERLOOKING THE LEARNING.**

FAMILY MINDFRAME 1:

I am an evaluator of my impact on my children's learning.

Impact is a powerful word. The question is, did your efforts to ensure that your child learned something actually result in learning? Was there an impact on their learning? Too much attention is spent on the processes and not enough on the outcomes. Do your homework. Get on the Zoom meeting. Pay attention to the teacher. Study. Those may be useful in impacting learning, but the question of impact has not yet been answered.

We shouldn't focus narrowly on grades while overlooking the learning. We want children to earn good grades. But those grades should reflect learning and not compliance. We're not suggesting that you can change a teacher's grading system. We have spent a great deal of time attempting to change the discussions in schools from the teaching to the learning.

At home, we ask the same of you. If you choose any of the strategies in Section 2 or 3 of this book, how will you know that they impacted your child's learning? If you require that your child complete a specific number of tasks, how will you know that they enhanced learning?

This mindframe requires that you shift your thinking from compliance on tasks, to the ways in which the tasks impact your child's learning. Remember:

➡ Ask your child what they learned and not what they did.

➡ Help your child monitor their progress toward goals.

➡ Have discussions about what they understand success could look like as they begin an activity.

➡ Talk more about the learning than the grades. Celebrate the effort and process.

➡ Choose something to learn yourself and model the ways in which you know that you are learning.

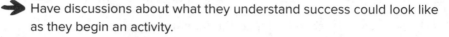

FAMILY MINDFRAME 2:

I see the power of collaborating with others in parenting our children.

The African proverb that it takes a village to raise a child speaks to the importance of collaboration in the emotional, psychological, and physical well-being of young people. This collaboration begins within the family from birth as parents and other caregivers learn to coordinate their viewpoints to create consistency. Children crave stability from the people they love and look to for guidance. It doesn't mean that everyone has to entirely agree on every point. However, the collective reliability of the caring adults in a child's life form a foundation of security that provides children with the confidence to try new things.

When formal schooling begins, the village gets a bit larger. Educators should partner with families for the common goal of expanding a child's academic identity and agency in ways that enhance his understanding of himself and the world. These partnerships are fostered in two ways: the openness of the school and the openness of the parent. This mindframe comes from the family side of the equation. The strengths you possess are tremendously influential. Student voice surveys repeatedly show that over

90 percent of students report that their families care about their education and name their families as personal heroes. And teachers want their students to do well in school and in life. We're not at cross purposes, but we don't always know how to talk to one another in ways that are growth-producing for all.

You might begin by introducing yourself to your child's teacher so as to establish a relationship—and even better to do this with your child involved. There's no need to wait until Back to School Night to meet the teacher. Drop a quick email or leave a voice message that includes your contact information. Sometimes teachers can be hesitant to approach a parent, so this sends a clear signal that you welcome the opportunity.

Model mutual respect for your child. Teachers know pedagogy and parents know parenting. While there is some overlap, it isn't one and the same. One of the very best things you can do is stand together with your child's teacher so that your child sees the teacher as part of the team.

Presume positive intentions when an assignment is problematic. Even when there is a conflict to be resolved, it is useful to approach the situations with the view that the teacher has your child's interests in mind. Work together to find solutions that are child centered, keeping in mind that sometimes the outcomes may be difficult for your child in the short term but instructive for her in the long term. Remember:

> **STAND TOGETHER WITH YOUR CHILD'S TEACHER SO THAT YOUR CHILD SEES THE TEACHER AS PART OF THE TEAM.**

- ➡ Consistent messages from the family and school create a stable and reliable space for your child to thrive.

- ➡ One of the very best things you can do for your child is to build their network. Your child's teachers are an important part of that team.

- ➡ Model for your child how you consider the viewpoints of others when working through a conflict at school. There is nothing to be gained from undermining the respect of your child for the school.

FAMILY MINDFRAME 3:

I value what my child brings to the family and world.

You are your children's advocate, encourager, guide, and protector. As an advocate, you seek out opportunities for them to grow. As an encourager, you console them when they are suffering and search for the life lessons that accompany many challenges. As a guide, you make sure they regularly try new things that stretch them, but you don't take the journey for them. And as their protector, you do your best to ensure their emotional and physical safety.

In doing so, you learn about who your children are through their responses to the world around them. Some children are shy and reserved while others are extroverts who are the center of attention everywhere they go. And these different personalities may co-exist in the same household. Each child brings unique value to your family and to the world. As a keeper of your child's history you have the singular viewpoint of watching them develop across many years.

The value each child brings is singular and isn't comparable to other children in the family or outside of it. Resist the urge to make comparisons to what other children are or aren't doing. Academically, many of the benchmark indicators represent an average, so there is a range broader than a single number can fully convey. Think more in terms of personal bests, and this will focus on each child's investment to exceed their previous best and keep improving. In the meantime, reinforce the value your child brings to the family in terms of their interests, skills, and insightfulness. Your child will carry your words with them throughout their life (even if you think they're not listening to you much at the moment).

Share with their teacher the ways your children are valued by your family. Educators catch only fleeting glimpses of who their students are outside of an academic setting. Tell the teacher that this child is kind to their younger siblings, shares the same sense of humor as their grandmother, and loves beating their older brother when they play board games. Those insights that only you know help the teacher to cultivate an appreciative eye of your child's caring and understand when they are a bit of a class clown or get a little too competitive with classmates. Remember:

➡ Each child possesses unique value to the family and the world.

➡ Other people's children are equally of value.

➡ Resist comparing children.

➡ Celebrate and share what they each bring.

FAMILY MINDFRAME 4:

I understand the centrality of my child.

Most parents would confess that there have been times when a child has done something amazing and you think to yourself, "He got that from me!" On the other hand, when he's not been the shining star you think, "He's just like _____", usually someone from the other parent's family. Taking pride in your child's accomplishments is one of the many rewards of parenting. But it is important to remember that each child is their own unique individual, and not clones of ourselves. Their accomplishments belong to them, and not to their parents. The same is true for their struggles.

We want the best for our children, but it is healthy for everyone involved to recognize the centrality of the individual. Parenting gone bad happens when a child is pushed hard to achieve something because the parent believes it reflects positively on them. Many of us have witnessed the fallout when a parent lives through their child. No child should have to bear the impossible responsibility of living up to their parent's dreams to the exclusion of their own. Whether it is getting into a university, earning a position on a sports team, or being elected to student government, these accomplishments belong to them. When the self-worth of an adult is drawn from a child, it steals the achievement from the young person. It belongs to them alone.

The same thing goes for their struggles. When children have difficulty socially or academically, be there to console and guide them. Discipline them fairly if that's what the situation warrants. But resist the urge to make it something you internalize about yourself. Children need acceptance in equal measure at their brightest and darkest moments. A parent who turns a child's imperfection into evidence of one's own defect damages the unconditional regard a young person needs from their family.

Remembering the centrality of the child as an individual and not as an extension of yourself protects your relationship with them. It preserves the joy they experience when they achieve a goal, allowing it to fuel their sense of agency. When they fail, the security you exhibit as an adult and a parent reminds them that you are there for them no matter what. Remember:

> Each child is a unique individual and separate from you.

> Their accomplishments belong to them, as do their struggles.

> Parents are there to guide, console, celebrate, and accept them. That's your superpower.

FAR TOO MANY PARENTS ARE UNDULY INFLUENCED BY REPORT CARDS AND GRADES.

FAMILY MINDFRAME 5:

I have appropriately high expectations.

High expectations are a powerful way to accelerate learning. In general, children rise to the expectations that they, and the people around them, have. It works in reverse as well. When there are minimal expectations, a child often accomplishes just that. Importantly, the expectations do need to be reasonable but challenging. The Goldilocks principle should drive the expectations we have for children—not too hard, not too easy, and not too boring.

Undoubtedly, your expectations have been influenced by your child's past performance. There's evidence for that as well. Past performance is a strong predictor of future performance, but it's not destiny. There are actions you and the teachers can take to change course. But you have to expect that learning will accelerate and then allocate resources (time, efforts) to accomplish that.

Far too many parents are unduly influenced by report cards and grades. Yes, you want to monitor these documents, but often these do not reflect the progress your child has made over time, and they are notoriously subjective. Don't let these reports reduce the expectations you have for your child.

There are two general types of goals, which are one way that we can express our expectations. The first is *mastery*, or the accomplishments we hope for children in terms of their learning. The second is *performance*, or the scores and grades that they earn. Mastery goals are much more powerful in ensuring learning.

Are you clear about the expectations you have for your child? Are these expectations focused on learning or on grades? Remember:

➡ Hold high, and reasonable, expectations for your children's learning.

➡ Don't be overly influenced by report cards and grades in terms of your expectations.

➡ Talk about your hopes and expectations for your child's learning.

➡ Help your child set mastery goals for learning.

FAMILY MINDFRAME 6:

I listen, build trust, and know how to gradually release responsibility.

There are three parts to this mindframe:

The first is listening. The opposite of speaking is not waiting to speak again; it's listening. In terms of your child's learning, they need you to listen. They need you to hear them and the language they use. Listening allows you to know what stuck with them and what they are confused about. And listening helps you understand your child's perspective on the world.

The second is trust. Trusting relationships are critical for growth. Trust involves age-appropriate honesty, reliability, and openness. When there is trust, children are more likely to take risks and feel comfortable making errors. And not just between you and your child. They look to see if you trust the teacher.

And last is gradually releasing responsibility. This is a framework for teaching that has been around for several decades. It's useful for you as well. Slowly but steadily increase the responsibility that your child has for learning. As they are able to assume that responsibility, you can give them more. And if there is a problem, you may have to take back some of that responsibility.

These three principles—listening, trust, and a gradual release of responsibility—are valuable characteristics of effective partnerships with the school. Parent–teacher partners who make the effort to listen carefully to one another are more productive.

The maxim to "seek to understand, before being understood" builds trust among the adults, thereby speeding up results. And look for the evolution of a gradual release of responsibility across the school year. As your child builds their skills, they need opportunities to apply them in increasingly independent ways. In order to do so, the teacher systematically shifts a greater amount of responsibility to the student to exercise those muscles. They may not always be successful in doing so, but those errors and missteps are an important way in which they become a more independent learner. Celebrate their successes and attempts.

Together, these three ensure that your child has the support necessary for learning. Without any one of these—being heard, developing trust, or increasing responsibility—your child's learning may suffer. Remember:

➡ Listening can signal when you need to take action.

➡ Listening tells your child that they are important.

➡ Trust facilitates bonding and ensures the child that they can make errors.

➡ Releasing responsibility demonstrates trust and expectations.

> **CHILDREN'S MAJOR SOURCES OF MEANINGFULNESS ARE THE FAMILY AND SCHOOL.**

FAMILY MINDFRAME 7:

I know the balancing act between developing autonomy, relatedness, and competence.

Humans seek meaningfulness throughout their lives. Children's major sources of meaningfulness are the family and school. Another way to understand meaningfulness is to view it as satisfaction. Young people who experience satisfaction at home and school

- See their choices as expressions of their authentic and valued selves
- Feel connected to others and understand that they are cared about by others
- Believe that their actions have a positive impact on others

These beliefs about oneself are interconnected and each enhances the other.

The first, **autonomy**, is fostered through the habit of being able to make choices that are reasonable and allow your child to reflect who they are. As an example, parents give toddlers opportunities to pick between clothing items, even when the results are somewhat unconventional.

The second, **relatedness**, is the belief on the part of the child that their actions and choices are supported by caring people. That sense of affinity and bonding forms the secure foundation that allows them to explore and try new things. Any parent who has sent a young child off to a new experience recognizes that the trembling lower lip indicates some anxiety that they overcome because they are secure that you will be there to support them.

The third is **competence**, which is belief that one's actions matter to others and are valued by people they care about. Competence is tied to mastery of a goal, whether it is setting the table or completing a college admissions application. We've discussed many times throughout this book the importance of helping children to set academic and nonacademic goals, as it contributes to a growing sense of their own competence to do more and appreciate their own progress.

As a parent it's a bit like being a plate spinner, trying to keep all of these going. Like the plate spinner, you are rapidly shifting your attention among the three, making decisions about how to build each while maintaining harmony among them. Sacrificing one means sacrificing all because a child who is weighed down by external pressures without any opportunity to exercise autonomy, who feels alone and disconnected from others, and who believes himself to be incompetent is at great risk for feeling a loss of meaning.

It's difficult to watch your child go down in defeat in a sport that he doesn't play very well. But celebrate the fact that he took a risk and made choices. You're there to comfort and encourage him because he is secure in your unconditional regard for him as a person. It isn't easy to witness your teenager select high school courses that aren't aligned to her goals, despite your advice. But understand that she is exploring her autonomy and actions, and in the aftermath of the regrets that she may suffer, you're there to counsel her about next steps.

It's all a balancing act, and no parent (or school) ever gets it 100 percent right every time, with every child. Remember:

➡ Provide lots of opportunities for developmentally appropriate choices to build autonomy.

➡ Help your child set goals and process their goal attainment and goal failure in equal measure.

➡ Unconditional regard is most important when your child struggles, but it might also be the time when they have trouble perceiving it. Make sure your children know you are there for them always.

➡ You don't expect perfection from your child. Extend that grace to yourself.

FAMILY MINDFRAME 8:

I appreciate the power of feedback and the place for praise as well as errors.

In Section 2, we discussed feedback in the context of academic learning. As we had noted, feedback is used to advance learning by bridging what a student currently does to that which he is not doing yet. The types of feedback that work especially well are feedback about the task, about the process, and the self-regulation required. Less effective, in the context of learning, is feedback about the individual as a person. Simply saying "You're awesome!" doesn't give the learner much guidance about what to do next.

In the context of parenting, praise is appropriate, especially in measured doses. The unconditional regard you hold for your child is expressed in part by the heaps of love you sprinkle on your child. When you do praise, make it matter by using it for things they can control, such as their effort and actions, and not for talent or ability. This can have the opposite of your intended effect, as it can cause a child to avoid challenge and stick only with what they already know how to do.

Expand your repertoire by providing effective feedback about nonacademic situations. The advantage to doing so is that it provides your child with knowledge about what they should stop, start, or continue doing. In other words, they can take action. "You did a good job with the dinner dishes—clean and dry!" (task). "It seems like you were in a hurry and didn't finish" (self-regulation). "Remember that the job's not done until they're put away" (process).

The errors they make in nonacademic situations contribute to their learning, especially if you provide the kind of feedback that moves them forward. Some people call it "constructive feedback" because it is action oriented and doesn't focus on the short-comings of the person. Remember:

> Use effective feedback to provide your child with information about what to start, stop, or continue doing.

> Love and encouragement are valuable; praise efforts and actions to give them room to embrace challenge.

> Naturalize errors by talking about your own and how you address them.

> WHEN YOU DO PRAISE, MAKE IT MATTER BY USING IT FOR THINGS THEY CAN CONTROL, SUCH AS THEIR EFFORT AND ACTIONS, AND NOT FOR TALENT OR ABILITY.

FAMILY MINDFRAME 9:

I know how to work with the school.

Schools are partners with you in your child's learning and as in any good partnership, each brings skills and strengths to the collaboration. Partners in any endeavor bring out the best in one another when there is mutual respect. The unique contributions of each amplify the efforts of the other.

Partnerships between families and schools provide a solid foundation for mutual growth. These partnerships are best built before there is any conflict; in practice that isn't always possible. However, even in conflict, partnerships can be forged. The National Parent Teacher Association offers guidelines for developing and maintaining ways for schools and families to work together in healthy and beneficial ways:

> Welcoming all families into the school community requires not only that schools create a productive climate but also that families are welcoming of one another. An inclusive climate depends on every member, including those with differing cultural, racial, economic, and family structures from your own.

➡️ **Effectively communicating** such that information is shared with one another, and that families seek to be active and engaged members of the school community. This looks different for every family and is not limited to those who are able to volunteer. Effective communication means that ideas and input are offered for the common good, not only on issues that directly impact your child.

➡️ **Supporting student success** requires that families provide children with the social, emotional, psychological, and physical nurturing that makes it possible for the school to build academic learning.

➡️ **Speaking up for every child** extends the previous standard. Families advocate for those who struggle to meet the needs of their children and partner with the school to attend to the needs of the most vulnerable.

➡️ **Sharing power** means that democratic principles of schooling are embodied in a willingness to debate ideas, listen to one another, and find win-win solutions.

➡️ **Collaborating with the community** is at the heart of working shoulder to shoulder with your child's school. The school as an organization is a manifestation of the community it serves, including those who do not have an enrolled child. The school is an arm of the community at large. As a member of the community, you use your voice to connect the school to resources. The school is also a member of the community and seeks to leverage community resources to benefit those it serves.

Remember:

➡️ Strong partnerships between you and the school are dependent on your willingness to do so.

➡️ Effective partnerships need honest and growth-producing communication that is oriented to finding mutually beneficial solutions.

➡️ Families advocate for their own children, other families, and the community at large.

FAMILY MINDFRAME 10:

I am a parent, not a schoolteacher.

You are your child's first and best teacher. Your child looks to you as a model of how to move through the world. Parenting is a huge undertaking that shapes a child's identity and actions. From you they learn the moral and ethical responsibilities that will guide them for the rest of their lives. We offer this mindframe as a reminder about the essential role you play in the life of your child. This mindframe is intended to encourage you to give the grace to yourself that you extend to others.

There are also people that you bring into your child's life because of the skills they possess. The pediatrician, the dentist, and the athletic coach each provide a service that improves your child's life in one form or another. Add teachers to that list of knowledgeable adults that play a part in your child's development. In the crisis teaching of spring 2020, parents did heroic things in partnership with schools to keep some semblance of learning happening. Now we want to lift some of that burden from your shoulders. Remember, a lot of the minutes spent in physical school focus on things your child already knows. Thus, there is time to ensure that your child learns what they need to.

The ideas throughout this book are intended to illuminate the important things you do to support your child's learning. They are ideas. We don't expect you to do them all. Importantly, we don't want you to feel as though you need to be your child's chemistry teacher, too. Distance learning that is planned and crafted with long-term outcomes in mind provides your child with a more coherent schooling experience. And your child will learn. Implement the basics from the first section, do what you can to assist in learning, ensure your child's well-being, and work to develop the mindframes in this final section. All will be well.

We encourage you to be comfortable asking for help from your child's teacher, school, or district. Your voice as a parent is crucial to improving schooling for all students. But we can't help if you don't say something. Be comfortable with saying to your child "I don't know" when she asks a question about a subject she's studying. Follow it up with, "How could you ask that question of your teacher?" If a teacher shares some data with you and it's not clear to you what it means, speak up and say, "Please explain this so I can understand what it says about my child's learning." As a parent, you already have a big job. Do the things that make a difference in your child's life and understand that you don't also need to be your child's chief reading, mathematics, social studies, science, and art teacher. Remember:

- A parent is a child's first and primary teacher.

- Allow yourself the grace to not be the go-to expert on everything.

- Professional teachers are positioned to provide their pedagogical knowledge to foster learning.

- Communicate with your child's teacher, school, and district about what is working and when you need help.

- Encourage your child to communicate with their teacher directly about their learning.

> **YOUR VOICE AS A PARENT IS CRUCIAL TO IMPROVING SCHOOLING FOR ALL STUDENTS. BUT WE CAN'T HELP IF YOU DON'T SAY SOMETHING.**

References

American Psychiatric Association. (2020, March). *New poll: COVID-19 impacting mental well-being: Americans feeling anxious, especially for loved ones; older adults are less anxious*. Retrieved from https://www.psychiatry.org/newsroom/news-releases/new-poll-covid-19-impacting-mental-well-being-americans-feeling-anxious-especially-for-loved-ones-older-adults-are-less-anxious

Anderson, R. C., Wilson, P. T., & Fielding, L. G. (1988). Growth in reading and how children spend their time outside of school. *Reading Research Quarterly, 23*(3), 285–303.

Fisher, D., & Frey, N. (2009). *Background knowledge: The missing piece of the comprehension puzzle*. Portsmouth, NH: Heinemann.

Fisher, D., Frey, N., & Hattie, J. (2017). *Teaching literacy in the visible learning classroom, grades K–5*. Thousand Oaks, CA: Corwin.

Fisher, D., Frey, N., & Hattie, J. (2020). *The distance learning playbook, grades K–12: Teaching for engagement and impact in any setting*. Thousand Oaks, CA: Corwin.

Fisher, D., Frey, N., Hattie, J., & Flories, K. (2019). *Becoming an assessment-capable visible learner, grades 3–5. Learner's notebook*. Thousand Oaks, CA: Corwin.

Heitner, D. (2020). *Tips for surviving remote school*. Retrieved from https://www.raisingdigitalnatives.com/wp-content/uploads/2020/08/Tips-for-surviving-remote-school-by-Devorah-Heitner-author-of-Screenwise-4-1-1.pdf

So, A. (2020). How to make remote learning work for your children. *Wired*. Retrieved from https://www.wired.com/story/remote-learning-school-coronavirus-tips/

Twenge, J. M. (2000). *The age of anxiety? Birth cohort change in anxiety and neuroticism, 1952–1993*. Retrieved from https://www.apa.org/pubs/journals/releases/psp7961007.pdf

Wiseman, R. (2020). *Owning up: Empowering adolescents to create cultures of dignity and confront social cruelty and injustice*. Thousand Oaks, CA: Corwin.

Yopp, H. K. (1995). A test for assessing phonemic awareness in young children. *Reading Teacher, 49*(1), 20–29.

Index

About the Authors

Rosalind Wiseman is a teacher, thought leader, and best-selling author of *Queen Bees & Wannabees*, the book that inspired the hit movie and musical *Mean Girls*; *Masterminds & Wingmen*; and *Owning Up: Empowering Adolescents to Create Cultures of Dignity and Confront Social Cruelty and Injustice,* Third Edition, a curriculum for middle and high school students. She is the founder of Cultures of Dignity and lives in Colorado with her husband and two children. Follow her on Twitter @cultureodignity.

Douglas Fisher, PhD, is a professor of educational leadership at San Diego State University and a leader at Health Sciences High & Middle College. He has served as a teacher, language development specialist, and administrator in public schools and nonprofit organizations. Doug has engaged in professional learning communities for several decades, building teams that design and implement systems to impact teaching and learning. He has published numerous books on teaching and learning, such as *The Distance Learning Playbook* and the *PLC+* series.

(Continued)

Nancy Frey, PhD, is a professor in educational leadership at San Diego State University and a leader at Health Sciences High & Middle College. She has been a special education teacher, reading specialist, and administrator in public schools. Nancy has engaged in professional learning communities as a member and in designing schoolwide systems to improve teaching and learning for all students. She has published numerous books, including *The Distance Learning Playbook, K–12* and *The Distance Learning Playbook for College and University Instruction.*

John Hattie, PhD, is an award-winning education researcher and best-selling author with nearly 30 years of experience examining what works best in student learning and achievement. His research, better known as Visible Learning, is a culmination of nearly 30 years synthesizing more than 1,500 meta-analyses comprising more than 90,000 studies involving over 300 million students around the world. His notable publications include *Visible Learning*, *Visible Learning for Teachers*, *Visible Learning and the Science of How We Learn*, and *10 Mindframes for Visible Learning.*

A SAGE Publishing Company

Helping educators make the greatest impact

CORWIN HAS ONE MISSION: to enhance education through intentional professional learning.

We build long-term relationships with our authors, educators, clients, and associations who partner with us to develop and continuously improve the best evidence-based practices that establish and support lifelong learning.